Frontispiece Vol.1.

W. Hogarth inv.t *Vol. 2. page 128.* *S. Ravenet Sculp.t*

THE
L I F E
AND
O P I N I O N S
OF
TRISTRAM SHANDY,
GENTLEMAN.

Ταράσσει τὲς Ἀνθρώπυς ἐ τὰ Πράϳμαϳα,
ἀλλὰ τὰ περὶ τῶν Πραϳμάτων, Δόϳμάτα.

VOL. I.
The SECOND EDITION.

L O N D O N:

Printed for R. and J. DODSLEY in *Pall-Mall*.
M.DCC.LX.

To the Right Honourable

Mr. P I T T.

SIR,

NEVER poor Wight of a Dedicator had lefs hopes from his Dedication, than I have from this of mine; for it is written in a bye corner of the kingdom, and in a retired thatch'd houfe, where I live in a conftant endeavour to fence againft the infirmities of ill health, and other evils of life, by

mirth;

mirth; being firmly perfuaded that every time a man fmiles, — but much more fo, when he laughs, that it adds fomething to this Frag- ment of Life.

I humbly beg, Sir, that you will honour this book by taking it ——(not under your Protection, ——it muft protect itfelf, but)— into the country with you; where, if I am ever told, it has made you fmile, or can conceive it has beguiled you of one moment's pain——I fhall think myfelf as happy as a minifter of ftate;——. perhaps much happier than any

one

DEDICATION.

one (one only excepted) that I have ever read or heard of.

I am, great Sir,

(and what is more to your Honour,)

I am, good Sir,

Your Well-wisher,

and most humble Fellow-Subject,

THE AUTHOR.

THE

LIFE and OPINIONS

OF

TRISTRAM SHANDY, Gent.

CHAP. I.

I Wish either my father or my mother,
or indeed both of them, as they
were in duty both equally bound to it,
had minded what they were about when
they begot me; had they duly confider'd
how much depended upon what they
were then doing;——that not only the
production of a rational Being was concern'd in it, but that poffibly the happy
formation and temperature of his body,

per-

perhaps his genius and the very caſt of his mind ;—and, for aught they knew to the contrary, even the fortunes of his whole houſe might take their turn from the humours and diſpoſitions which were then uppermoſt :——Had they duly weighed and conſidered all this, and proceeded accordingly,——I am verily perſuaded I ſhould have made a quite different figure in the world, from that, in which the reader is likely to ſee me.— Believe me, good folks, this is not ſo inconſiderable a thing as many of you may think it ;—you have all, I dare ſay, heard of the animal ſpirits, as how they are transfuſed from father to ſon, &c. &c.— and a great deal to that purpoſe :—Well, you may take my word, that nine parts in ten of a man's ſenſe or his nonſenſe, his ſucceſſes and miſcarriages in this world depend upon their motions and ac-

tivity,

tivity, and the different tracks and trains you put them into, so that when they are once set a-going, whether right or wrong, 'tis not a halfpenny matter,—away they go cluttering like hey-go-mad; and by treading the same steps over and over again, they presently make a road of it, as plain and as smooth as a garden-walk, which, when they are once used to, the Devil himself sometimes shall not be able to drive them off it.

Pray, my dear, quoth my mother, *have you not forgot to wind up the clock?*——*Good G—!* cried my father, making an exclamation, but taking care to moderate his voice at the same time,——*Did ever woman, since the creation of the world, interrupt a man with such a silly question?* Pray, what was your father saying?——Nothing.

A 2　　　　CHAP.

C H A P. II.

——Then, pofitively, there is nothing in the queftion, that I can fee, either good or bad.——Then let me tell you, Sir, it was a very unfeafonable queftion at leaft,—becaufe it fcattered and difperfed the animal fpirits, whofe bufinefs it was to have efcorted and gone hand-in-hand with the *HOMUNCULUS*, and conducted him fafe to the place deftined for his reception.

The HOMUNCULUS, Sir, in how-ever low and ludicrous a light he may appear, in this age of levity, to the eye of folly or prejudice :—to the eye of reafon in fcientifick refearch, he ftands confefs'd— a BEING guarded and circumfcribed with rights :——The minuteft philofophers, who,

who, by the bye, have the moſt enlarged underſtandings, (their ſouls being inverſely as their enquiries) ſhew us inconteſtably, That the HOMUNCULUS is created by the ſame hand,—engender'd in the ſame courſe of nature,—endowed with the ſame loco-motive powers and faculties with us :——That he conſiſts, as we do, of ſkin, hair, fat, fleſh, veins, arteries, ligaments, nerves, cartileges, bones, marrow, brains, glands, genitals, humours, and articulations ;——is a Being of as much activity,——and, in all ſenſes of the word, as much and as truly our fellow-creature as my Lord Chancellor of England.—He may be benefited, he may be injured,—he may obtain redreſs ;—in a word, he has all the claims and rights of humanity, which *Tully*, *Puffendorff*, or the beſt ethick writers

allow

allow to arife out of that ftate and relation.

Now, dear Sir, what if any accident had befallen him in his way alone?——or that, thro' terror of it, natural to fo young a traveller, my little gentleman had got to his journey's end miferably fpent;——his mufcular ftrength and virility worn down to a thread;——his own animal fpirits ruffled beyond defcription,——and that in this fad diforder'd ftate of nerves, he had laid down a prey to fudden ftarts, or a feries of melancholy dreams and fancies for nine long, long months together.——I tremble to think what a foundation had been laid for a thoufand weakneffes both of body and mind, which no fkill of the phyfician or the philofopher could ever afterwards have fet thoroughly to rights.

CHAP.

CHAP. III.

TO my uncle Mr. *Toby Shandy* do I
stand indebted for the preceding
anecdote, to whom my father, who was
an excellent natural philofopher, and
much given to clofe reafoning upon the
fmalleft matters, had oft, and heavily,
complain'd of the injury; but once more
particularly, as my uncle *Toby* well remember'd, upon his obferving a moft
unaccountable obliquity, (as he call'd it)
in my manner of fetting up my top, and
juftifying the principles upon which I
had done it,—the old gentleman fhook
his head, and in a tone more expreffive
by half of forrow than reproach,—he faid
his heart all along foreboded, and he
faw it verified in this, and from a thoufand other obfervations he had made up-

on

on me, That I ſhould neither think nor act like any other man's child :——*But alas!* continued he, ſhaking his head a ſecond time, and wiping away a tear which was trickling down his cheeks, *My Triſtram's misfortunes began nine months before ever he came into the world.*

——My mother, who was ſitting by, look'd up,—but ſhe knew no more than her backſide what my father meant,—but my uncle, Mr. *Toby Shandy,* who had been often informed of the affair,—un- derſtood him very well.

C H A P. IV.

I Know there are readers in the world, as well as many other good people in it, who are no readers at all,—who
find

find themselves ill at ease, unless they are, let into the whole secret from first to last, of every thing which concerns you.

It is in pure compliance with this humour of theirs, and from a backwardness in my nature to disappoint any one soul living, that I have been so very particular already. As my life and opinions are likely to make some noise in the world, and, if I conjecture right, will take in all ranks, professions, and denominations of men whatever,—be no less read than the *Pilgrim's Progress* itself—and, in the end, prove the very thing which *Montaigne* dreaded his essays should turn out, that is, a book for a parlour-window ;—I find it necessary to consult every one a little in his turn ; and therefore must beg pardon for going on a little further in the same way : For which cause, right glad

I

I am, that I have begun the hiftory of myfelf in the way I have done; and that I am able to go on tracing every thing in it, as *Horace* fays, *ab Ovo.*

Horace, I know, does not recommend this fafhion altogether : But that gentleman is fpeaking only of an epic poem or a tragedy ;—(I forget which)—befides, if it was not fo, I fhould beg Mr. *Horace's* pardon ;—for in writing what I have fet about, I fhall confine myfelf neither to his rules, nor to any man's rules that ever lived.

To fuch, however, as do not choofe to go fo far back into thefe things, I can give no better advice, than that they fkip over the remaining part of this Chapter; for I declare before hand, 'tis

wrote

wrote only for the curious and inquiſi-
tive.

—————————Shut the door.———————

I was begot in the night, betwixt the firſt
Sunday and the firſt *Monday* in the month
of *March*, in the year of our Lord one
thouſand ſeven hundred and eighteen.
I am poſitive I was.—But how I came
to be ſo very particular in my account
of a thing which happened before I was
born, is owing to another ſmall anecdote
known only in our own family, but now
made publick for the better clearing up
this point.

My father, you muſt know, who was
originally a *Turkey* merchant, but had left
off buſineſs for ſome years, in order to
retire to, and die upon, his paternal eſtate
in the county of————, was, I believe,

2   one

one of the moſt regular men in every
thing he did, whether 'twas matter of
buſineſs, or matter of amuſement, that
ever lived. As a ſmall ſpecimen of this
extreme exactneſs of his, to which he
was in truth a ſlave,—he had made it a
rule for many years of his life,—on the
firſt *Sunday night* of every month throughout the whole year,—as certain as ever
the *Sunday night* came,——to wind up a
large houſe-clock which we had ſtanding
upon the back-ſtairs head, with his own
hands :—And being ſomewhere between
fifty and ſixty years of age, at the time I
have been ſpeaking of,—he had likewiſe
gradually brought ſome other little family concernments to the ſame period,
in order, as he would often ſay to my
uncle *Toby*, to get them all out of the
way at one time, and be no more plagued

and

and pefter'd with them the reft of the
month.

It was attended but with one misfortune, which, in a great meafure, fell upon
myfelf, and the effects of which I fear
I fhall carry with me to my grave;
namely, that, from an unhappy affociation
of ideas which have no connection in nature, it fo fell out at length, that my
poor mother could never hear the faid
clock wound up,—but the thoughts of
fome other things unavoidably popp'd
into her head,—*& vice verfâ* :—which
ftrange combination of ideas, the faga-
cious *Locke*, who certainly underftood
the nature of thefe things better than
moft men, affirms to have produced
more wry actions than all other fources
of prejudice whatfoever.

But this by the bye.

Now

Now it appears, by a memorandum in my father's pocket-book, which now lies upon the table, " That on *Lady-Day*, which was on the 25th of the same month in which I date my geniture,—my father set out upon his journey to *London* with my eldest brother *Bobby*, to fix him at *Westminster* school;" and, as it appears from the same authority, " That he did not get down to his wife and family till the *second week* in *May* following,"—it brings the thing almost to a certainty. However, what follows in the beginning of the next chapter puts it beyond all possibility of doubt.

————But pray, Sir, What was your father doing all *December*,—*January*, and *February* ?————Why, Madam,—he was all that time afflicted with a Sciatica.

CHAP.

CHAP. V.

ON the fifth day of *November*, 1718, which to the æra fixed on, was as near nine kalendar months as any hufband could in reafon have expeƈted,—was I *Triftram Shandy*, Gentleman, brought forth into this fcurvy and difafterous world of ours.—I wifh I had been born in the Moon, or in any of the planets, (except *Jupiter* or *Saturn*, becaufe I never could bear cold weather) for it could not well have fared worfe with me in any of them (tho' I will not anfwer for *Venus*) than it has in this vile, dirty planet of ours,—which o' my confcience, with reverence be it fpoken, I take to be made up of the fhreds and clippings of the reft;——not but the planet is well enough, provided a man could be born

in it to a great title or to a great estate;
or could any how contrive to be called
up to publick charges, and employments
of dignity or power;—but that is not
my case;———and therefore every man
will speak of the fair as his own market
has gone in it;—for which cause I affirm
it over again to be one of the vilest
worlds that ever was made;—for I can
truly say, that from the first hour I drew
my breath in it, to this, that I can now
scarce, draw it at all, for an asthma I got
in scating against the wind in *Flanders*;—
I have been the continual sport of what
the world calls fortune; and though I
will not wrong her by saying, She has
ever made me feel the weight of any
great or signal evil;—yet with all the
good temper in the world, I affirm it of
her, that in every stage of my life, and
ate very turn and corner where she could

get

get fairly at me, the ungracious Duchefs
has pelted me with a fet of as pitiful
mifadventures and crofs accidents as ever
fmall HERO fuftained.

C H A P. VI.

IN the beginning of the laft chapter,
I inform'd you exactly *when* I was
born;—but I did not inform you, *how.*
No; that particular was referved entirely
for a chapter by itfelf;—befides, Sir, as
you and I are in a manner perfect ftran-
gers to each other, it would not have been
proper to have let you into too many
circumftances relating to myfelf all at
once.—You muft have a little patience.
I have undertaken, you fee, to write not
only my life, but my opinions alfo; ho-
ping and expecting that your knowledge

VOL. I.   B   of

of my character, and of what kind of a
mortal I am, by the one, would give you
a better relish for the other: As you
proceed further with me, the slight ac-
quaintance which is now beginning betwixt us, will grow into familiarity ; and
that, unless one of us is in fault, will
terminate in friendship.——*O diem præ-
clarum !*——then nothing which has
touched me will be thought trifling in
its nature, or tedious in its telling.
Therefore, my dear friend and compa-
nion, if you should think me somewhat
sparing of my narrative on my first setting
out,—bear with me,—and let me go on,
and tell my story my own way :——or
if I should seem now and then to trifle
upon the road,——or should sometimes
put on a fool's cap with a bell to it, for
a moment or two as we pass along,—don't
fly off,—but rather courteously give me
credit

credit for a little more wifdom than appears upon my outfide;—and as we jogg on, either laugh with me, or at me, or in fhort, do any thing,—only keep your temper.

C H A P. VII.

IN the fame village where my father and my mother dwelt, dwelt alfo a thin, upright, motherly, notable, good old body of a midwife, who, with the help of a little plain good fenfe, and fome years full employment in her bufinefs, in which fhe had all along trufted little to her own efforts, and a great deal to thofe of dame nature,—had acquired, in her way, no fmall degree of reputation in the world;—by which word *world*, need I in this place inform your worfhip,

that

that I would be underftood to mean no
more of it, than a fmall circle defcribed
upon the circle of the great world, of
four *Englifh* miles diameter, or thereabouts, of which the cottage where the
good old woman lived, is fuppofed to be
the centre.——She had been left it,
feems, a widow in great diftrefs, with
three or four fmall children, in her forty-
feventh year; and as fhe was at that time
a perfon of decent carriage,—grave deportment,——a woman moreover of few
words, and withall an object of compaffion, whofe diftrefs and filence under it
call'd out the louder for a friendly lift:
the wife of the parfon of the parifh was
touch'd with pity ; and having often lamented an inconvenience, to which her
hufband's flock had for many years been
expofed, inafmuch, as there was no fuch
thing as a midwife, of any kind or degree

gree to be got at, let the cafe have been never fo urgent, within lefs than fix or feven long miles riding; which faid feven long miles in dark nights and difmal roads, the country thereabouts being nothing but a deep clay, was almoft equal to fourteen; and that in effect was fometimes next to having no midwife at all; it came into her head, that it would be doing as feafonable a kindnefs to the whole parifh, as to the poor creature herfelf, to get her a little inftructed in fome of the plain principles of the bufinefs, in order to fet her up in it. As no woman thereabouts was better qualified to execute the plan fhe had formed than herfelf, the Gentlewoman very charitably undertook it; and having great influence over the female part of the parifh, fhe found no difficulty in effecting it to the utmoft of her wifhes. In truth, the parfon join'd his intereft

with

with his wife's in the whole affair ; and
in order to do things as they fhould be,
and give the poor foul as good a title by
law to practife, as his wife had given by
inftitution,——he chearfully paid the
fees for the ordinaries licence himfelf,
amounting, in the whole, to the fum of
eighteen fhillings and fourpence ; fo that,
betwixt them both, the good woman
was fully invefted in the real and corpo-
ral poffeffion of her office, together with
all its *rights, members, and appurtenances
whatfoever.*

. Thefe laft words, you muft know,
were not according to the old form in
which fuch licences, faculties, and powers
ufually ran, which in like cafes had heretofore been granted to the fifterhood.
But it was according to a neat *Formula*
of *Didius* his own devifing, who having.

a

a particular turn for taking to pieces, and new framing over again, all kind of inftruments in that way, not only hit upon this dainty amendment, but coax'd many of the old licenfed matrons in the neighbourhood, to open their faculties afrefh, in order to have this whim-wham of his inferted.

I own I never could envy *Didius* in thefe kinds of fancies of his :—But every man to his own tafte.—Did not Dr. *Kunaftrokius*, that great man, at his leifure hours, take the greateft delight imaginable in combing of affes tails, and plucking the dead hairs out with his teeth, though he had tweezers always in his pocket ? Nay, if you come to that, Sir, have not the wifeft of men in all ages, not excepting *Solomon* himfelf,—have they not had their HOBBY-HORSES ;—their running

horfes,

horfes,—their coins and their cockle-
fhells, their drums and their trumpets,
their fiddles, their pallets,——their maggots and their butterflies?—and fo long
as a man rides his HOBBY-HORSE peaceably and quietly along the King's high-
way, and neither compels you or me to
get up behind him,——pray, Sir, what
have either you or I to do with it?

C H A P. VIII.

—*Deguftibus non eft difputandum;*—that
is, there is no difputing againft HOBBY-
HORSES; and, for my part, I feldom do;
nor could I with any fort of grace, had
I been an enemy to them at the bottom; for happening, at certain intervals
and changes of the Moon, to be both
fiddler and painter, according as the fly
ftings:—Be it known to you, that I

keep

keep a couple of pads myfelf, upon which, in their turns, (nor do I care who knows it) I frequently ride out and take the air;—tho' fometimes, to my fhame be it fpoken, I take fomewhat longer journies than what a wife man would think altogether right.—But the truth is,—I am not a wife man ;———and befides am a mortal of fo little confequence in the world, it is not much matter what I do ; fo I feldom fret or fume at all about it : Nor does it much difturb my reft when I fee fuch great Lords and tall Perfonages as hereafter follow ;—fuch, for inftance, as my Lord A, B, C, D, E, F, G, H, I, K, L, M, N, O, P, Q, and fo on, all of a row, mounted upon their feveral horfes;—fome with large ftirrups, getting on in a more grave and fober pace ;———others on the contrary, tuck'd up to their very chins, with whips acrofs

their

their mouths, fcouring and fcampering
it away like fo many little party-colour'd
devils aftride a mortgage,——and as if
fome of them were refolved to break
their necks.—So much the better—fay
I to myfelf;—for in cafe the worft fhould
happen, the world will make a fhift to do
excellently well without them;—and
for the reft,——why,——God fpeed
them,——e'en let them ride on without
oppofition from me; for were their lord-
fhips unhorfed this very night,——'tis
ten to one but that many of them would
be worfe mounted by one half before to-
morrow morning.

Not one of thefe inftances therefore
can be faid to break in upon my reft.—
But there is an inftance, which I own puts
me off my guard, and that is, when I fee
one born for great actions, and, what is
.ftill

ftill more for his honour, whofe nature
ever inclines him to good ones ;———
when I behold fuch a one, my Lord, like
yourfelf, whofe principles and conduct
are as generous and noble as his blood,
and whom, for that reafon, a corrupt
world cannot fpare one moment ;—when
I fee fuch a one, my Lord, mounted,
though it is but for a minute beyond the
time which my love to my country has
prefcribed to him, and my zeal for his
glory wifhes,—then, my Lord, I ceafe
to be a philofopher, and in the firft
tranfport of an honeft impatience, I wifh
the Hobby-Horse, with all his frater-
nity, at the Devil.

My Lord,

" I Maintain this to be a dedication,
" notwithftanding its fingularity in
" the three great effentials of matter,
" form,

" form and place: I beg, therefore, you
" will accept it as fuch, and that you will
" permit me to lay it, with the moft re-
" fpectful humility, at your Lordfhip's
" feet,—when you, are upon them,—
" which you can be when you pleafe;—
" and that is, my Lord, when ever there
" is occafion for it, and I will add, to the
" beft purpofes too. I have the honour
" to be,

My Lord,

Your Lordfhip's moft obedient,

and moft devoted,

and moft humble fervant,

TRISTRAM SHANDY.

CHAP.

C H A P. IX.

I Solemnly declare to all mankind, that the above dedication was made for no one Prince, Prelate, Pope, or Potentate,—Duke, Marquis, Earl, Vifcount, or Baron of this, or any other Realm in Chriftendom ;——nor has it yet been hawk'd about, or offered publickly or privately, directly or indirectly, to any one perfon or perfonage, great or fmall; but is honeftly a true Virgin-Dedication untried on, upon any foul living.

I labour this point fo particularly, merely to remove any offence or objection which might arife againft it, from the manner in which I propofe to make the moft of it ;—which is the putting

it

it up fairly to publick fale; which I now do.

——Every author has a way of his own, in bringing his points to bear;—for my own part, as I hate chaffering and higgling for a few guineas in a dark entry;—I refolved within myfelf, from the very beginning, to deal fquarely and openly with your Great Folks in this af-fair, and try whether I fhould not come off the better by it.

If therefore there is any one Duke, Marquis, Earl, Vifcount, or Baron, in thefe his Majefty's dominions, who ftands in need of a tight, genteel dedication, and whom the above will fuit, (for by the bye, unlefs it fuits in fome degree, I will not part with it)——it is much at his fervice for fifty guineas;——which

I

I am pofitive is twenty guineas lefs than
it ought to be afforded for, by any man
of genius.

My Lord, if you examine it over
again, it is far from being a grofs piece
of daubing, as fome dedications are.
The defign, your Lordfhip fees, is good,
the colouring tranfparent,—the drawing
not amifs;—or to fpeak more like a man
of fcience,—and meafure my piece in the
painter's fcale, divided into 20,—I believe, my Lord, the out-lines will turn
out as 12,—the compofition as 9,—the
colouring as 6,—the expreffion 13 and
a half,—and the defign,—if I may be
allowed, my Lord, to underftand my own
defign, and fuppofing abfolute perfecti-
on in defigning, to be as 20,—I think it
cannot well fall fhort of 19. Befides
all this,—there is keeping in it, and
the

the dark ſtrokes in the HOBBY-HORSE,
(which is a ſecondary figure, and a kind
of back-ground to the whole) give great
force to the principal lights in your own
figure, and make it come off wonder-
fully ;——and beſides, there is an air of
originality in the *tout enſemble.*

Be pleaſed, my good Lord, to order
the ſum to be paid into the hands of Mr.
Dodſley, for the benefit of the author ;
and in the next edition care ſhall be taken that this chapter be expunged, and
your Lordſhip's titles, diſtinctions, arms
and good actions, be placed at the front
of the preceding chapter : All which,
from the words, *De guſtibus non eſt diſpu-
tandum*, and whatever elſe in this book
relates to HOBBY-HORSES, but no more,
ſhall ſtand dedicated to your Lordſhip.—
The reſt I dedicate to the MOON, who, by
the

the bye, of all the PATRONS or MATRONS
I can think of, has moſt power to ſet my
book a-going, and make the world run
mad after it.

Bright Goddeſs,

If thou art not too buſy with CANDID
and Miſs CUNEGUND's affairs,—take *Triſtram Shandy*'s under thy protection alſo.

CHAP. X.

WHatever degree of ſmall merit,
the act of benignity in favour of
the midwife, might juſtly claim, or in
whom that claim truly reſted,—at firſt
ſight ſeems not very material to this
hiſtory ;——certain however it was, that
the gentlewoman, the parſon's wife, did
run away at that time with the whole
of it: And yet, for my life, I cannot help
thinking but that the parſon himſelf,

tho'

tho' he had not the good fortune to hit upon the defign firſt,—yet, as he heartily concurred in it the moment it was laid before him, and as heartily parted with his money to carry it into execution, had a claim to fome fhare of it,—if not to a full half of whatever honour was due to it.

The world at that time was pleafed to determine the matter otherwife.

Lay down the book, and I will allow you half a day to give a probable guefs at the grounds of this procedure.

Be it known then, that, for about five years before the date of the midwife's licence, of which you have had fo cir-cumftantial an account,—the parfon we have to do with, had made himfelf a

country-

country-talk by a breach of all decorum,
which he had committed againſt himſelf,
his ſtation, and his office ;——and that
was, in never appearing better, or otherwiſe mounted, than upon a lean, ſorry,
jack-aſs of a horſe, value about one
pound fifteen ſhillings ; who, to ſhorten
all deſcription of him, was full brother to
Roſinante, as far as ſimilitude congenial
could make him ; for he anſwered his
deſcription to a hair-breadth in every
thing,——except that I do not remember
'tis any where ſaid, that *Roſinante* was
broken winded ; and that, moreover, *Roſi-*
nante, as is the happineſs of moſt *Spaniſh*
horſes, fat or lean,——was uudoubtedly a
horſe at all points.

I know very well that the Hero's
horſe was a horſe of chaſte deportment,
which may have given grounds for a

con-

contrary opinion : But it is as certain at
the fame time, that *Rofinante*'s continen-
cy (as may be demonftrated from the ad-
venture of the *Yanguefian* carriers) proceeded from no bodily defect or caufe
whatfoever, but from the temperance
and orderly current of his blood.—And
let me tell you, Madam, there is a great
deal of very good chaftity in the world,
in behalf of which you could not fay
more for your life.

Let that be as it may, as my purpofe
is to do exact juftice to every creature
brought upon the ftage of this dramatic
work,—I could not ftifle this diftinction
in favour of Don *Quixote*'s horfe;———in
all other points the parfon's horfe, I fay,
was juft fuch another,———for he was as
lean, and as lank, and as forry a jade, as
HUMILITY herfelf could have beftrided.

In

In the eſtimation of here and there a man of weak judgment, it was greatly in the parſon's power to have helped the figure of this horſe of his,—for he was maſter of a very handſome demi-peak'd ſaddle, quilted on the ſeat with green pluſh, garniſhed with a double row of ſilver-headed ſtuds, and a noble pair of ſhining braſs ſtirrups, with a houſing altogether ſuitable, of grey ſuperfine cloth, with an edging of black lace, terminating in a deep, black, ſilk fringe, *poudrè d'or*,—all which he had purchaſed in the pride and prime of his life, together with a grand emboſſed bridle, ornamented at all points as it ſhould be.——But not caring to banter his beaſt, he had hung all theſe up behind his ſtudy door;—and, in lieu of them, had ſeriouſly befitted him with juſt ſuch a bridle and ſuch

a

a faddle, as the figure and value of fuch
a fteed might well and truly deferve.

In the feveral fallies about his parifh,
and in the neighbouring vifits to the
gentry who lived around him,———you
will eafily comprehend, that the parfon,
fo appointed, would both hear and fee
enough to keep his philofophy from
rufting. To fpeak the truth, he never
could enter a village, but he caught the
attention of both old and young.———Labour ftood ftill as he pafs'd,———the bucket
hung fufpended in the middle of the
well,———the fpinning-wheel forgot its
round,———even chuck-farthing and
fhuffle-cap themfelves ftood gaping till
he had got out of fight; and as his
movement was not of the quickeft, he
had generally time enough upon his
hands to make his obfervations,———to hear

the

the groans of the ferious,——and the
laughter of the light-hearted ;——all which
he bore with excellent tranquility.—His
character was,——he loved a jeft in his
heart—and as he faw himfelf in the true
point of ridicule, he would fay, he could
not be angry with others for feeing him
in a light, in which he fo ftrongly faw
himfelf: So that to his friends, who
knew his foible was not the love of money, and who therefore made the lefs
fcruple in bantering the extravagance of
his humour,—inftead of giving the true
caufe,——he chofe rather to join in the
laugh againft himfelf; and as he never
carried one fingle ounce of flefh upon his
own bones, being altogether as fpare a
figure as his beaft,—he would fometimes
infift upon it, that the horfe was as good
as the rider deferved ;—that they were,
centaur-like,—both of a piece. At other

C 4   times,

times, and in other moods, when his
spirits were above the temptation of false
wit,—he would say, he found himself
going off fast in a consumption ; and,
with great gravity, would pretend, he
could not bear the sight of a fat horse
without a dejection of heart, and a sensi-
ble alteration in his pulse ; and that he
had made choice of the lean one he rode
upon, not only to keep himself in countenance, but in spirits.

At different times he would give fifty
humourous and opposite reasons for riding a meek-spirited jade of a broken-
winded horse, preferably to one of met-
tle ;—for on such a one he could sit me-
chanically, and meditate as delightfully
de vanitate mundi et fugâ sæculi, as with
the advantage of a death's head before
him ;—that, in all other exercitations, he
could

could spend his time, as he rode slowly
along,——to as much account as in his
study;——that he could draw up an argument in his sermon,—or a hole in his
breeches, as steadily on the one as in the
other;—that brisk trotting and slow ar-
gumentation, like wit and judgment, were
two incompatible movements.—But that
upon his steed—he could unite and reconcile every thing,—he could compose
his sermon,—he could compose his
cough,——and, in case nature gave a
call that way, he could likewise compose
himself to sleep.—In short, the parson
upon such encounters would assign any
cause, but the true cause,—and he with-
held the true one, only out of a nicety of
temper, because he thought it did honour to him.

But

But the truth of the story was as follows: In the firſt years of this gentleman's life, and about the time when the
ſuperb ſaddle and bridle were purchaſed
by him, it had been his manner, or va-
nity, or call it what you will,——to run
into the oppoſite extream.——In the lan-
guage of the county where he dwelt, he
was ſaid to have loved a good horſe, and
generally had one of the beſt in the whole
pariſh ſtanding in his ſtable always ready
for ſaddling; and as the neareſt midwife,
as I told you, did not live nearer to the
village than ſeven miles, and in a vile
country,——it ſo fell out that the poor
gentleman was ſcarce a whole week together without ſome piteous application
for his beaſt; and as he was not an un-
kind-hearted man, and every caſe was
more preſſing and more diſtreſsful than
the laſt,——as much as he loved his beaſt,

he

he had never a heart to refuse him ; the
upſhot of which was generally this, that
his horſe was either clapp'd, or ſpavin'd,
or greaz'd ;—or he was twitter-bon'd, or
broken-winded, or ſomething, in ſhort,
or other had befallen him which would
let him carry no fleſh ;—ſo that he had
every nine or ten months a bad horſe to
get rid of,—and a good horſe to purchaſe
in his ſtead.

What the loſs in ſuch a balance might
amount to, *communibus annis*, I would leave
to a ſpecial jury of ſufferers in the ſame
traffic, to determine ;—but let it be what
it would, the honeſt gentleman bore it
for many years without a murmur, till
at length, by repeated ill accidents of the
kind, he found it neceſſary to take the
thing under conſideration ; and upon
weighing the whole, and ſumming it up
in

in his mind, he found it not only difpro-
portion'd to his other expences, but
withall fo heavy an article in itfelf, as to
difable him from any other act of gene-
rofity in his parifh : Befides this he con-
fidered, that with half the fum thus gal-
loped away, he could do ten times as
much good ;———and what ftill weighed
more with him than all other confiderations put together, was this, that it confined all his charity into one particular
channel, and where, as he fancied, it was
the leaft wanted, namely, to the child-
bearing and child-getting part of his
parifh ; referving nothing for the impo-
tent,—nothing for the aged,—nothing
for the many comfortlefs fcenes he was
hourly called forth to vifit, where poverty, and ficknefs, and affliction dwelt
together.

For

For thefe reafons he refolved to dif-
continue the expence; and there appeared but two poffible ways to extricate
him clearly out of it;—and thefe were,
either to make it an irrevocable law never more to lend his fteed upon any application whatever,—or elfe be content
to ride the laft poor devil, fuch as they
had made him, with all his aches and in-
firmities, to the very end of the chapter.

As he dreaded his own conftancy in
the firft,——he very chearfully betook
himfelf to the fecond; and tho' he could
very well have explain'd it, as I faid, to
his honour,—yet, for that very reafon, he
had a fpirit above it; choofing rather to
bear the contempt of his enemies, and
the laughter of his friends, than undergo
the pain of telling a ftory, which might
feem a panegyric upon himfelf.

I

I have the higheſt idea of the ſpiritual
and refined ſentiments of this reverend
gentleman, from this ſingle ſtroke in his
character, which I think comes up to any
of the honeſt refinements of the peerleſs
knight of *La Mancha*, whom, by the
bye, with all his follies, I love more, and
would actually have gone further to have
paid a viſit to, than the greateſt hero of
antiquity.

But this is not the moral of my ſtory:
The thing I had in view was to ſhew the
temper of the world in the whole of this
affair.——For you muſt know, that ſo long
as this explanation would have done the
parſon credit,——the devil a ſoul could find
it out,——I ſuppoſe his enemies would not,
and that his friends could not.——But
no ſooner did he beſtir himſelf in behalf
of the midwife; and pay the expences of
the

the ordinary's licence to set her up,—but the whole secret came out; every horse he had lost, and two horses more than ever he had lost, with all the circumstances of their destruction, were known and distinctly remembered.—The story ran like wild-fire. — "The parson had "a returning fit of pride which had just "seized him; and he was going to be "well mounted once again in his life; "and if it was so, 'twas plain as the sun "at noon-day, he would pocket the ex-"pence of the licence, ten times told the "very first year :——so that every body "was left to judge what were his views "in this act of charity."

What were his views in this, and in every other action of his life,—or rather what were the opinions which floated in the brains of other people concerning it,
was

was a thought which too much floated in
his own, and too often broke in upon his
reft, when he fhould have been found
afleep.

About ten years ago this gentleman
had the good fortune to be made entirely
eafy upon that fcore,——it being juft fo
long fince he left his parifh,——and the
whole world at the fame time behind
him,—and ftands accountable to a judge
of whom he will have no caufe to complain.

But there is a fatality attends the actions of fome men: Order them as they
will, they pafs thro' a certain medium
which fo twifts and refracts them from
their true directions——that, with
all the titles to praife which a rectitude
of heart can give, the doers of them are
ne-

nevertheleſs forced to live and die without it.

Of the truth of which this gentleman
was a painful example.——But to know
by what means this came to paſs,—and
to make that knowledge of uſe to you,
I inſiſt upon it that you read the two following chapters, which contain ſuch a
ſketch of his life and converſation, as
will carry its moral along with it.—When
this is done, if nothing ſtops us in our
way, we will go on with the midwife.

C H A P. XI.

YORICK was this parſon's name, and,
what is very remarkable in it, (as
appears from a moſt antient account of
the family, wrote upon ſtrong vellum,

and now in perfect prefervation) it had
been exactly fo fpelt for near,——I was
within an ace of faying nine hundred
years ;——but I would not fhake my
credit in telling an improbable truth,
however indifputable in itfelf ;——and
therefore I fhall content myfelf with only faying,—It had been exactly fo fpelt,
without the leaft variation or tranfpofi-
tion of a fingle letter, for I do not know
how long ; which is more than I would
venture to fay of one half of the beft furnames in the kingdom ; which, in a courfe
of years, have generally undergone as
many chops and changes as their own-
ers.—Has this been owing to the pride,
or to the fhame of the refpective propri-
etors ?—In honeft truth, I think, fometimes to the one, and fometimes to the
other, juft as the temptation has wrought.
But a villainous affair it is, and will one

day

day fo blend and confound us all together, that no one fhall be able to ftand up and fwear, " That his own great grand fa-" ther was the man who did either this " or that."

This evil had been fufficiently fenced againft by the prudent care of the *Yorick*'s family, and their religious prefervation of thefe records I quote, which do fur-ther inform us, That the family was ori-ginally of *Danifh* extraction, and had been tranfplanted into *England* as early as in the reign of *Horwendillus*, king of *Denmark*, in whofe court it feems, an anceftor of this Mr. *Yorick*'s, and from whom he was lineally defcended, held a confider-able poft to the day of his death. Of what nature this confiderable poft was, this record faith not;—it only adds, That, for near two centuries, it had been totally

abo-

abolished as altogether unnecessary, not only in that court, but in every other court of the Christian world.

It has often come into my head, that this post could be no other than that of the king's chief Jester;—and that *Hamlet*'s *Yorick*, in our *Shakespear*, many of whose plays, you know, are founded upon authenticated facts,—was certainly the very man.

I have not the time to look into *Saxo-Grammaticus*'s *Danish* history, to know the certainty of this;—but if you have leisure, and can easily get at the book, you may do it full as well yourself.

I had just time, in my travels through *Denmark* with Mr. *Noddy*'s eldest son, whom, in the year 1741, I accompanied

as

as governor, riding along with him at a
prodigious rate thro' moſt parts of *Europe*,
and of which original journey perform'd
by us two, a moſt delectable narrative
will be given in the progreſs of this work.
I had juſt time, I ſay, and that was all, to
prove the truth of an obſervation made
by a long ſojourner in that country ;——
namely, " That nature was neither very
laviſh, nor was ſhe very ſtingy in her
gifts of genius and capacity to its inhabitants ;—but, like a diſcreet parent, was
moderately kind to them all ; obſerving
ſuch an equal tenor in the diſtribution of
her favours, as to bring them, in thoſe
points, pretty near to a level with each
other; ſo that you will meet with few in-
ſtances in that kingdom of refin'd parts;
but a great deal of good plain houſhold
underſtanding amongſt all ranks of

D 3   people,

people, of which every body has a fhare;"
which is, I think, very right.

With us, you fee, the cafe is quite
different;—we are all ups and downs in
this matter;—you are a great genius;—
or 'tis fifty to one, Sir, you are a great
dunce and a blockhead;—not that there
is a total want of intermediate fteps,—
no,—we are not fo irregular as that comes
to;—but the two extremes are more
common, and in a greater degree in this
unfettled ifland, where nature, in her gifts
and difpofitions of this kind, is moft
whimfical and capricious; fortune herfelf not being more fo in the bequeft of
her goods and chattels than fhe.

This is all that ever ftagger'd my faith
in regard to *Yorick*'s extraction, who, by
what I can remember of him, and by all
the

the accounts I could ever get of him, seem'd not to have had one single drop of *Danish* blood in his whole crasis; in nine hundred years, it might possibly have all run out :———I will not philosophize one moment with you about it; for happen how it would, the fact was this :— That instead of that cold phlegm and exact regularity of sense and humours, you would have look'd for, in one so extracted ;—he was, on the contrary, as mercurial and sublimated a composition,— as heteroclite a creature in all his declensions ;——with as much life and whim, and *gaité de cœur* about him, as the kindliest climate could have engendered and put together. With all this sail, poor *Yorick* carried not one ounce of ballast; he was utterly unpractised in the world; and, at the age of twenty-six, knew just about as well how to steer his course

D 4   in

in it, as a romping, unſuſpicious girl of
thirteen: So that upon his firſt ſetting
out, the briſk gale of his ſpirits, as you
will imagine, ran him foul ten times in
a day of ſome body's tackling; and as
the grave and more ſlow-paced were
ofteneſt in his way,———you may likewiſe imagine, 'twas with ſuch he had
generally the ill luck to get the moſt en-
tangled. For aught I know there might
be ſome mixture of unlucky wit at the
bottom of ſuch *Fracas:*——For, to ſpeak
the truth, *Yorick* had an invincible diſ-
like and oppoſition in his nature to gravity;———not to gravity as ſuch;———for
where gravity was wanted, he would be
the moſt grave or ſerious of mortal men
for days and weeks together;—but he
was an enemy to the affectation of it,
and declared open war againſt it, only as
it appeared a cloak for ignorance, or for
folly:

folly ; and then, whenever it fell in his way, however sheltered and protected, he seldom gave it much quarter.

. Sometimes, in his wild way of talking, he would say, That gravity was an errant scoundrel ; and he would add,—of the most dangerous kind too,—because a sly one ; and that, he verily believed, more honest, well-meaning people were bubbled out of their goods and money by it in one twelve-month, than by pocket-picking and shop-lifting in seven. In the naked temper which a merry heart discovered, he would say, There was no danger,—but to itself:—whereas the very essence of gravity was design, and consequently deceit ;—'twas a taught trick to gain credit of the world for more sense and knowledge than a man was worth ; and that, with all its pretensions,—it was

no

no better, but often worfe, than what a *French* wit had long ago defined it,—*viz.* *A myfterious carriage of the body to cover the defects of the mind* ;—which definition of gravity, *Yorick*, with great imprudence, would fay, deferved to be wrote in letters of gold.

But, in plain truth, he was a man unhackneyed and unpractifed in the world, and was altogether as indifcreet and foolifh on every other fubject of difcourfe where policy is wont to imprefs reftraint. *Yorick* had no impreffion but one, and that was what arofe from the nature of the deed fpoken of ; which impreffion he would ufually tranflate into plain *Englifh* without any periphrafis,—— and too oft without much diftinction of either perfonage, time, or place ;—fo that when mention was made of a pitiful or an

un-

ungenerous proceeding,—he never gave himself a moment's time to reflect who was the Hero of the piece,——what his station,——or how far he had power to hurt him hereafter;—but if it was a dirty action,——without more ado,——The man was a dirty fellow,—and so on :—— And as his comments had usually the ill fate to be terminated either in a *bon mot*, or to be enliven'd throughout with some drollery or humour of expression, it gave wings to *Yorick*'s indiscretion. In a word, tho' he never sought, yet, at the same time, as he seldom shun'd occasions of saying what came uppermost, and without much ceremony;——he had but too many temptations in life, of scattering his wit and his humour,—his gibes and his jests about him.——They were not lost for want of gathering.

What

What were the confequences, and
what was *Yorick*'s cataftrophe thereupon, you will read in the next chapter.

C H A P. XII.

THE *Mortgager* and *Mortgagée*
differ the one from the other, not
more in length of purfe, than the *Jefter*
and *Jeftée* do, in that of memory. But
in this the comparifon between them
runs, as the fcholiafts call it, upon all-
four; which, by the bye, is upon one
or two legs more, than fome of the beft
of *Homer*'s can pretend to ;—namely,
That the one raifes a fum and the other
a laugh at your expence, and think no
more about it. Intereft, however, ftill
runs on in both cafes ;—the periodical
or accidental payments of it, juft ferving

to keep the memory of the affair alive;
till, at length, in fome evil hour,—pop
comes the creditor upon each, and by
demanding principal upon the fpot, together with full intereft to the very day,
makes them both feel the full extent of
their obligations.

As the reader (for I hate your *ifs*) has
a thorough knowledge of human nature,
I need not fay more to fatisfy him, that
my Hero could not go on at this rate
without fome flight experience of thefe
incidental mementos. To fpeak the
truth, he had wantonly involved himfelf
in a multitude of fmall book-debts of
this ftamp, which, notwithftanding *Eugenius*'s frequent advice, he too much
difregarded; thinking, that as not one
of them was contracted thro' any malig-
nancy;—but, on the contrary, from an
honefty

honefty of mind, and a mere jocundity
of humour, they would all of them be
crofs'd out in courfe.

Eugenius would never admit this; and
would often tell him, that one day or
other he would certainly be reckoned
with; and he would often add, in an ac-
cent of forrowful apprehenfion,—to the
uttermoft mite. To which Yorick, with
his ufual carelefnefs of heart, would as
often anfwer with a pfhaw!—and if the
fubject was ftarted in the fields,—with a
hop, fkip, and a jump; at the end of it;
but if clofe pent up in the focial chimney
corner, where the culprit was barrica-
do'd in, with a table and a couple of
arm chairs, and could not fo readily fly
off in a tangent,—Eugenius would then
go on with his lecture upon difcretion, in
words

'words to this purpose, though somewhat better put together.

Trust me, dear *Yorick*, this unwary pleasantry of thine will sooner or later bring thee into scrapes and difficulties, which no after-wit can extricate thee out of.——In these sallies, too oft, I see, it happens, that a person laugh'd at, considers himself in the light of a person injured, with all the rights of such a situation belonging to him ; and when thou viewest him in that light too, and reckons up his friends, his family, his kindred and allies,——and musters up with them the many recruits which will list under him from a sense of common danger ;——'tis no extravagant arithmetic to say, that for every ten jokes,——thou hast got a hundred enemies; and till thou hast gone on, and raised a swarm of wasps

about

about thy ears, and art half ftung to death by them, thou wilt never be convinced it is fo.

I cannot fufpect it in the man whom I efteem, that there is the leaft fpur from fpleen or malevolence of intent in thefe fallies.———I believe and know them to be truly honeft and fportive :—But confider, my dear lad, that fools cannot diftinguifh this,—and that knaves will not; and thou knoweft not what it is, either to provoke the one, or to make merry with the other,—whenever they affociate for mutual defence, depend upon it, they will carry on the war in fuch a manner againft thee, my dear friend, as to make thee heartily fick of it, and of thy life too.

REVENGE from fome baneful corner fhall level a tale of difhonour at thee,
which

which no innocence of heart or integrity of conduct fhall fet right.——The for-tunes of thy houfe fhall totter,—thy cha-racter, which led the way to them, fhall bleed on every fide of it,—thy faith que-ftioned,—thy works belied,—thy wit forgotten,—thy learning trampled on. To wind up the laft fcene of thy tragedy, CRUELTY and COWARDICE, twin ruf-fians, hired and fet on by MALICE in the dark, fhall ftrike together at all thy in-firmities and miftakes:—the beft of us, my dear lad, lye open there,—and truft me,—truft me, *Yorick, When to gratify a private appetite, it is once refolved up-on, that an innocent and an helplefs creature fhall be facrificed, 'tis an eafy matter to pick up fticks enew from any thicket where it has ftrayed, to make a fire to offer it up with.*

VOL. I.   E   *Yorick*

Yorick scarce ever heard this sad va-
ticination of his deftiny read over to him,
but with a tear ftealing from his eye, and
a promiffory look attending it, that he
was refolved, for the time to come, to
ride his tit with more fobriety.—But,
alas, too late!—a grand confederacy,
with ***** and ***** at the head of
it, was form'd before the firft prediction
of it.—The whole plan of the attack,
juft as *Eugenius* had foreboded, was put
in execution all at once,—with fo little
mercy on the fide of the allies,—and fo
little fufpicion in *Yorick,* of what was
carrying on againft him,—that when he
thought, good eafy man! full furely pre-
ferment was o'ripening,—they had fmote
his root, and then he fell, as many a
worthy man had fallen before him.

Yorick,

Yorick, however, fought it out with all imaginable gallantry for fome time; till, over-power'd by numbers, and worn out at length by the calamities of the war,—but more fo, by the ungenerous manner in which it was carried on,—he threw down the fword; and though he kept up his fpirits in appearance to the laft,—he died, neverthelefs, as was generally thought, quite broken hearted.

What inclined *Eugenius* to the fame opinion, was as follows:

A few hours before *Yorick* breath'd his laft, *Eugenius* ftept in with an intent to take his laft fight and laft farewell of him: Upon his drawing *Yorick*'s curtain, and afking how he felt himfelf, *Yorick*, looking up in his face, took hold of his hand,—and, after thanking him

for

for the many tokens of his friendſhip to
him, for which, he ſaid, if it was their
fate to meet hereafter,—he would thank
him again and again.—He told him, he
was within a few hours of giving his
enemies the ſlip for ever.—I hope not,
anſwered *Eugenius*, with tears trickling
down his cheeks, and with the tendereſt
tone that ever man ſpoke,—I hope not,
Yorick, ſaid he.—*Yorick* replied, with a
look up, and a gentle ſqueeze of *Eugenius's* hand, and that was all,—but it
cut *Eugenius* to his heart.—Come,—
come, *Yorick*, quoth *Eugenius*, wiping
his eyes, and ſummoning up the man
within him,—my dear lad, be comfort-
ed,—let not all thy ſpirits and fortitude
forſake thee at this criſis when thou moſt
wants them ;——who knows what re-
ſources are in ſtore, and what the power
of God may yet do for thee?——*Yorick*
laid

laid his hand upon his heart, and gently
shook his head;—for my part, continued *Eugenius*, crying bitterly as he uttered
the words,—I declare I know not, *Yorick*, how to part with thee,——and
would gladly flatter my hopes, added
Eugenius, chearing up his voice, that
there is still enough left of thee to make
a bishop,—and that I may live to see
it.——I beseech thee, *Eugenius*, quoth
Yorick, taking off his night-cap as well
as he could with his left hand,——his
right being still grasped close in that of
Eugenius,——I beseech thee to take a
view of my head.—I see nothing that
ails it, replied *Eugenius*. Then, alas!
my friend, said *Yorick*, let me tell you,
that 'tis so bruised and mif-shapen'd with
the blows which ***** and *****,
and some others have so unhandsomely
given me in the dark, that I might say

with *Sancho Pança,* that fhould I reco-
ver, and " Mitres thereupon be fuffer'd
" to rain down from heaven as thick as
" hail, not one of 'em would fit it."——
Yorick's laft breath was hanging upon
his trembling lips ready to depart as he
uttered this;—yet ftill it was utter'd
with fomething of a *cervantick* tone;—
and as he fpoke it, *Eugenius* could perceive a ftream of lambent fire lighted up
for a moment in his eyes;—faint picture
of thofe flafhes of his fpirit, which (as
Shakefpear faid of his anceftor) were wont
to fet the table in a roar!

Eugenius was convinced from this,
that the heart of his friend was broke;
he fqueez'd his hand, —— and then
walk'd foftly out of the room, weeping
as he walk'd. *Yorick* followed *Eugenius*
with his eyes to the door,—he then
clofed

clofed them,—and never opened them
more.

He lies buried in a corner of his
church-yard, in the parifh of ————,
under a plain marble flabb, which his
friend *Eugenius*, by leave of his executors,
laid upon his grave, with no more than
thefe three words of infcription ferving
both for his epitaph and elegy.

Alas, poor YORICK!

Ten times in a day has *Yorick*'s ghoft
the confolation to hear his monumental
infcription read over with fuch a variety
of plaintive tones, as denote a general

pity

pity and esteem for him;——a foot-
way crossing the church-yard close by
the side of his grave,—not a passenger
goes by without stopping to cast a look
upon it,——and sighing as he walks
on,

Alas, poor Y O R I C K !

C H A P. XIII.

IT is fo long fince the reader of this rhapfodical work has been parted from the midwife, that it is high time to mention her again to him, merely to put him in mind that there is fuch a body ftill in the world, and whom, upon the beft judgment I can form upon my own plan at prefent,—I am going to intro- duce to him for good and all: But as frefh matter may be ftarted, and much unexpected bufinefs fall out betwixt the reader and myfelf, which may require immediate difpatch;——'twas right to take care that the poor woman fhould not be loft in the mean time;—becaufe when fhe is wanted, we can no way do without her.

I

I think I told you that this good woman was à perſon of no ſmall note and
conſequence throughout our whole village and townſhip ;—that her fame had
ſpread itſelf to the very out-edge and cir-
cumference of that circle of importance,
of which kind every ſoul living, whether
he has a ſhirt to his back or no,——has
one ſurrounding him ;—which ſaid circle,
by the way, whenever 'tis ſaid that ſuch
a one is of great weight and importance
in the *world*,——I deſire may be enlarged or contracted in your worſhip's fancy, in a compound-ratio of the ſtation,
profeſſion, knowledge, abilities, height
and depth (meaſuring both ways) of the
perſonage brought before you.

In the preſent caſe, if I remember, I
fixed it at about four or five miles, which
not only comprehended the whole pariſh,

rifh, but extended itself to two or three
of the adjacent hamlets in the fkirts of
the next parifh ; which made a confider-
able thing of it. I muſt add, That ſhe
was, moreover, very well looked on at
one large grange-houſe and ſome other
odd houſes and farms within two or
three miles, as I ſaid, from the ſmoke of
her own chimney :———But I muſt here,
once for all, inform you, that all this will
be more exactly delineated and explain'd
in a map, now in the hands of the en-
graver, which, with many other pieces
and developments to this work, will be
added to the end of the twentieth volume,—not to ſwell the work,—I deteſt
the thought of ſuch a thing ;———but by
way of commentary, ſcholium, illuſtra-
tion, and key to ſuch paſſages, incidents,
or inuendos as ſhall be thought to be either of private interpretation, or of dark

or

or doubtful meaning after my life and my opinions fhall have been read over, (now don't forget the meaning of the word) by all the *world* ;—which, betwixt you and me, and in fpight of all the gentlemen reviewers in *Great-Britain*, and of all that their worfhips fhall undertake to write or fay to the contrary,—— I am determined fhall be the cafe,——I need not tell your worfhip, that all this is fpoke in confidence.

C H A P. XIV.

UPON looking into my mother's marriage fettlement, in order to fatisfy myfelf and reader in a point neceffary to be clear'd up, before we could proceed any further in this hiftory ;—I had the good fortune to pop upon the

.very

very thing I wanted before I had read a
day and a half ftraight forwards,—it
might have taken me up a month;—which
fhews plainly, that when a man fits down
to write a hiftory,—tho' it be but the hiftory of *Jack Hickathrift* or *Tom Thumb*,
he knows no more than his heels what
lets and confounded hinderances he is to
meet with in his way,—or what a dance
he may be led, by one excurfion or another, before all is over. Could a hifto-
riographer drive on his hiftory, as a
muleteer drives on his mule,—ftraight
forward;——for inftance, from *Rome* all
the way to *Loretto*, without ever once
turning his head afide either to the right
hand or to the left,—he might venture
to foretell you to an hour when he fhould.
get to his journey's end;——but the.
thing is, morally fpeaking, impoffible:
For, if he is a man of the leaft fpirit, he,
will

will have fifty deviations from a ftraight
line to make with this or that party as he
goes along, which he can no ways avoid.
He will have views and profpects to
himfelf perpetually folliciting his eye,
which he can no more help ftanding ftill
to look at than he can fly; he will moreover have various

 Accounts to reconcile :
 Anecdotes to pick up :
 Infcriptions to make out :
 Stories to weave in :
 Traditions to fift :
 Perfonages to call upon :
 Panegyricks to pafte up at this door :
 Pafquinades at that :——All which
both the man and his mule are quite ex-
empt from. To fum up all ; there are
archives at every ftage to be look'd in-
to, and rolls, records, documents, and
endlefs genealogies, which juftice ever
        and

and anon calls him back to ſtay the reading of :——In ſhort, there is no end of it ;——for my own part, I declare I have been at it theſe ſix weeks, making all the ſpeed I poſſibly could,—and am not yet born :—I have juſt been able, and that's all, to tell you *when* it happen'd, but not *how* ;—ſo that you ſee the thing is yet far from being accompliſhed.

Theſe unforeſeen ſtoppages, which I own I had no conception of when I firſt ſet out ;—but which, I am convinced now, will rather increaſe than diminiſh as I advance,—have ſtruck out a hint which I am reſolved to follow ;—and that is,— not to be in a hurry ;—but to go on lei- ſurely, writing and publiſhing two vo- lumes of my life every year ;——which, if I am ſuffered to go on quietly, and can make a tolerable bargain with my book-

VOL. I.   F   ſeller,

feller, I fhall continue to do as long as I live.

C H A P. XV.

THE article in my mother's marriage fettlement, which I told the reader I was at the pains to fearch for, and which, now that I have found it, I think proper to lay before him,—is fo much more fully exprefs'd in the deed itfelf, than ever I can pretend to do it, that it would be barbarity to take it out of the lawyer's hand :—It is as follows.

" **And this Indenture further**
" **witneffeth**, That the faid *Walter*
" *Shandy*, merchant, in confideration of
" the faid intended marriage to be had,
" and, by God's bleffing, to be well and

5   " truly

" truly folemnized and confummated be-
" tween the faid *Walter Shandy* and *Eli-*
" *zabeth Mollineux* aforefaid, and divers
" other good and valuable caufes and
" confiderations him thereunto fpecially
" moving,—doth grant, covenant, con-
" defcend, confent, conclude, bargain,
" and fully agree to and with *John Dixon*
" and *James Turner*, Efqrs. the above-
" named truftees, *&c. &c.*—**to wit,**—
" That in cafe it fhould hereafter fo fall
" out, chance, happen, or otherwife
" come to pafs,—That the faid *Walter*
" *Shandy*, merchant, fhall have left off
" bufinefs before the time or times, that
" the faid *Elizabeth Mollineux* fhall, ac-
" cording to the courfe of nature, or
" otherwife, have left off bearing and
" bringing forth children;—and that,
" in confequence of the faid *Walter Shan-*
" *dy* having fo left off bufinefs, fhall,

" in

" in defpight, and againſt the free-will,
" confent, and good-liking of the ſaid
" *Elizabeth Mollineux,*—make a depar-
" ture from the city of *London,* in order
" to retire to, and dwell upon, his eſtate
" at *Shandy-Hall,* in the county of——,
" or at any other country feat, caſtle, hall,
" manſion-houſe, meſſuage, or grainge-
" houſe, now purchaſed, or hereafter to
" be purchaſed, or upon any part or
" parcel thereof :—That then, and as of-
" ten as the ſaid *Elizabeth Mollineux* ſhall
" happen to be enceint with child or
" children feverally and lawfully begot,
" or to be begotten, upon the body of
" the faid *Elizabeth Mollineux* during her
" faid coverture,——he the ſaid *Walter*
" *Shandy* ſhall, at his own proper coſt
" and charges, and out of his own pro-
" per monies, upon good and reaſonable
" notice, which is hereby agreed to be
                                  " within

" within fix weeks of her the faid *Eliza-*
" *beth Mollineux*'s full reckoning, or
" time of fuppofed and computed deli-
" very,—pay, or caufe to be paid, the
" fum of one hundred and twenty pounds
" of good and lawful money, to *John*
" *Dixon* and *James Turner*, Efqrs. or af-
" figns,—upon TRUST and confidence,
" and for and unto the ufe and ufes, in-
" tent, end, and purpofe following :—
" 𝕿𝖍𝖆𝖙 𝖎𝖘 𝖙𝖔 𝖘𝖆𝖞,—That the faid fum
" of one hundred and twenty pounds
" fhall be paid into the hands of the faid
" *Elizabeth Mollineux*, or to be otherwife
" applied by them the faid truftees, for
" the well and truly hiring of one coach,
" with able and fufficient horfes, to car-
" ry and convey the body of the faid
" *Elizabeth Mollineux* and the child or
" children which fhe fhall be then and
" there enceint and pregnant with,—

" unto

" unto the city of *London* ; and for the
" further paying and defraying of all
" other incidental cofts, charges, and ex-
" pences whatfoever,—in and about;
" and for, and relating to her faid in-
" tended delivery and lying-in, in the
" faid city or fuburbs thereof. And that
" the faid *Elizabeth Mollineux* fhall and
" may, from time to time; and at all fuch
" time and times as are here covenant-
" ed and agreed upon,—peaceably and
" quietly hire the faid coach and horfes;
" and have free ingrefs, egrefs, and
" regrefs throughout her journey, in and
" from the faid coach, according to the
" tenor, true intent, and meaning of thefe
" prefents, without any let, fuit, trouble,
" difturbance, moleftation, difcharge;
" hinderance, forfeiture, eviction, vexa-
" tion, interruption, or incumberance
" whatfoever.—And that it fhall more-
" over

" over be lawful to and for the said *Eli-*
" *zabeth Mollineux,* from time to time,
" and as oft or often as she shall well and
" truly be advanced in her said pregnan-
" cy, to the time heretofore stipulated
" and agreed upon,—to live and reside
" in such place or places, and in such
" family or families, and with such rela-
" tions, friends, and other persons with-
" in the said city of *London,* as she, at
" her own will and pleasure, notwith-
" standing her present coverture, and as
" if she was a *femme sole* and unmarri-
" ed,—shall think fit.—𝕬𝖓𝖉 𝖙𝖍𝖎𝖘 𝕴𝖓=
" 𝖉𝖊𝖓𝖙𝖚𝖗𝖊 𝖋𝖚𝖗𝖙𝖍𝖊𝖗 𝖜𝖎𝖙𝖓𝖊𝖘𝖘𝖊𝖙𝖍,
" That for the more effectually carrying
" of the said covenant into execution, the
" said *Walter Shandy,* merchant, doth here-
" by grant, bargain, sell, release, and con-
" firm unto the said *John Dixon,* and
" *James Turner,* Esqrs. their heirs, exe-

" cutors,

" cutors, and affigns, in their actual pof-
" feffion, now being by virtue of an in-
" denture of bargain and fale for a year
" to them the faid *John Dixon* and *James*
" *Turner*, Efqrs. by him the faid *Walter*
" *Shandy*, merchant, thereof made; which
" faid bargain and fale for a year, bears
" date the day next before the date of
" thefe prefents, and by force and vir-
" tue of the ftatute for transferring of
" ufes into poffeffion,———𝕬𝖑𝖑 that
" the manor and lordfhip of *Shandy* in
" the county of———, with all the
" rights, members, and appurtenances
" thereof; and all and every the mef-
" fuages, houfes, buildings, barns, fta-
" bles, orchards, gardens, backfides,
" tofts, crofts, garths, cottages, lands,
" meadows, feedings, paftures, marfhes,
" commons, woods, underwoods, drains,
" fifheries, waters, and water-courfes;—
" to-

" together with all rents, reverſions, fer-
" vices, annuities, fee-farms, knights
" fees, views of frank-pledge, eſcheats;
" reliefs, mines, quarries, goods and
" chattels of felons and fugitives, felons
" of themſelves, and put in exigent,
" deodands, free warrens, and all other
" royalties and ſeignories, rights and ju-
" riſdictions, privileges and heredita-
" ments whatſoever.———**And alſo** the
" advowſon, donation, preſentation and
" free diſpoſition of the rectory or par-
" ſonage of *Shandy* aforeſaid, and all and
" every the tenths, tythes, glebe-lands"
———In three words,———" My mother
" was to lay in, (if ſhe choſe it) in
" *London.*"

But in order to put a ſtop to the practice of any unfair play on the part of my
mother, which a marriage article of this
nature,

nature too manifeftly opened a door to;
and which indeed had never been thought
of at all, but for my uncle *Toby Shandy*;——
a claufe was added in fecurity of my father, which was this:——" That in cafe my
" mother hereafter fhould, at any time,
" put my father to the trouble and ex-
" pence of a *London* journey upon falfe
" cries and tokens ;——that for every
" fuch inftance fhe fhould forfeit all the
" right and title which the covenant gave
" her to the next turn ;——but to no
" more,——and fo on, *toties quoties*, in as
" effectual a manner, as if fuch a co-
" venant betwixt them had not been
" made."——This, by the way, was no
more than what was reafonable ;——and
yet, as reafonable as it was, I have ever
thought it hard that the whole weight of
the article fhould have fallen entirely, as
it did, upon myfelf.

But

But I was begot and born to misfortunes;—for my poor mother, whether it was wind or water,—or a compound of both,—or neither;—or whether it was fimply the mere fwell of imagination and fancy in her;—or how far a ftrong wifh and defire to have it fo, might miflead her judgment;—in fhort, whether fhe was deceived or deceiving in this matter, it no way becomes me to decide. The fact was this, That, in the latter end of *September*, 1717, which was the year before I was born, my mother having carried my father up to town much againft the grain,—he peremptorily infifted upon the claufe;—fo that I was doom'd, by marriage articles, to have my nofe fqueez'd as flat to my face, as if the deftinies had actually fpun me without one.

How

How this event came about,—and what a train of vexatious disappointments, in one stage or other of my life, have pursued me from the mere loss, or rather compression, of this one single member,—shall be laid before the reader all in due time.

C H A P. XVI.

MY father, as any body may naturally imagine, came down with my mother into the country, in but a pettish kind of a humour. The first twenty or five-and-twenty miles he did nothing in the world but fret and teaze himself, and indeed my mother too, about the cursed expence, which he said might every shilling of it have been saved;— then what vexed him more than every

thing

thing elfe was the provoking time of the year,——which, as I told you, was towards the end of *September*, when his wall-fruit, and green gages efpecially, in which he was very curious, were juft ready for pulling:——" Had he been " whiftled up to *London*, upon a *Tom* " *Fool*'s errand in any other month of " the whole year, he fhould not have " faid three words about it."

For the next two whole ftages, no fubject would go down, but the heavy blow he had fuftain'd from the lofs of a fon, whom it feems he had fully reckon'd upon in his mind, and regifter'd down in his pocket-book, as a fecond ftaff for his old age, in cafe *Bobby* fhould fail him. " The difappointment of this, he faid, " was ten times more to a wife man than " all the money which the journey, &c. " had

" had coft him, put together,—rot the
" hundred and twenty pounds,——he
" did not mind it a rufh."

From *Stilton*, all the way to *Grantham*,
nothing in the whole affair provoked
him fo much as the condolences of his
friends, and the foolifh figure they fhould
both make at church the firft *Sunday* ;
——of which, in the fatirical-vehemence
of his wit, now fharpen'd a little by vex-
ation, he would give fo many humorous
and provoking defcriptions,—and place
his rib and felf in fo many tormenting
lights and attitudes in the face of the
whole congregation ;—that my mother
declared, thefe two ftages were fo truly
tragi-comical, that fhe did nothing but
laugh and cry in a breath, from one end
to the other of them all the way.

From

From *Grantham*, till they had crofs'd
the *Trent*, my father was out of all kind
of patience at the vile trick and impofition which he fancied my mother had
put upon him in this affair.—" Certainly,
he would fay to himfelf, over and over
again, " the woman could not be deceived herfelf ;——if fhe could, ———
what weaknefs !——tormenting word !
which led his imagination a thorny
dance, and, before all was over, play'd
the duce and all with him ;"——for
fure as ever the word *weaknefs* was uttered, and ftruck full upon his brain,—
fo fure it fet him upon running divi-
fions upon how many kinds of weakneffes there were ;——that there was
fuch a thing as weaknefs of the body,
——as well as weaknefs of the mind,—
and then he would do nothing but fyl-
logize within himfelf for a ftage or two

to-

together, How far the caufe of all thefe vexations might, or might not, have arifen out of himfelf.

In fhort, he had fo many little fubjects of difquietude fpringing out of this one affair, all fretting fucceffively in his mind as they rofe up in it, that my mother, whatever was her journey up, had but an uneafy journey of it down.——— In a word, as fhe complained to my uncle *Toby*, he would have tired out the patience of any flefh alive.

C H A P. XVII.

THough my father travelled home-wards, as I told you, in none of the beft of moods,—pfhaw-ing and pifh-ing all the way down,—yet he had the

com-

complaifance to keep the worft part of the ftory ftill to himfelf;—which was the refolution he had taken of doing himfelf the juftice, which my uncle *Toby's* claufe in the marriage fettlement empowered him; nor was it till the very night in which I was begot, which was thirteen months after, that fhe had the leaft intimation of his defign;—when my father, happening, as you remember, to be a little chagrin'd and out of temper,——took occafion as they lay chatting gravely in bed afterwards, talking over what was to come,——to let her know that fhe muft accommodate herfelf as well as fhe could to the bargain made between them in their marriage deeds; which was to lye-in of her next child in the country to balance the laft year's journey.

My father was a gentleman of many, virtues,—but he had a ſtrong ſpice of that in his temper which might, or might not, add to the number.—'Tis known by the name of perſeverance in a good cauſe,—and of obſtinacy in a bad one: Of this my mother had ſo much know-ledge, that ſhe knew 'twas to no pur-poſe to make any remonſtrance,—ſo ſhe e'en reſolved to ſit down quietly, and make the moſt of it.

C H A P. XVIII.

AS the point was that night agreed, or rather determin'd, that my mo-ther ſhould lye-in of me in the country, ſhe took her meaſures accordingly ; for which purpoſe, when ſhe was three days, or thereabouts, gone with child, ſhe be-

gan

gan to caſt her eyes upon the midwife,
whom you have ſo often heard me mention; and before the week was well got
round, as the famous Dr. *Maningham* was
not to be had, ſhe had come to a final
determination in her mind,——notwithſtanding there was a ſcientifick operator
within ſo near a call as eight miles of us,
and who, moreover, had expreſsly wrote
a five ſhillings book upon the ſubject of
midwifery, in which he had expoſed,
not only the blunders of the ſiſterhood
itſelf,——but had likewiſe ſuperadded
many curious improvements for the
quicker extraction of the fœtus in croſs
births, and ſome other caſes of danger
which belay us in getting into the world;
notwithſtanding all this, my mother, I
ſay, was abſolutely determined to truſt her
life and mine with it, into no ſoul's hand
but this old woman's only.—Now this I

G 2   like;

like ;—when we cannot get at the very
thing we wish,——never to take up
with the next beſt in degree to it ;—no ;
that's pitiful beyond deſcription ;—it is
no more than a week from this very day,
in which I am now writing this book for
the edification of the world,—which is
March 9, 1759,——that my dear, dear
Jenny obſerving I look'd a little grave,
as ſhe ſtood cheapening a ſilk of five-and-
twenty ſhillings a yard,—told the mer-
cer, ſhe was ſorry ſhe had given him ſo
much trouble ;—and immediately went
and bought herſelf a yard-wide ſtuff of
ten-pence a yard.—'Tis the duplication
of one and the ſame greatneſs of ſoul ;
only what leſſen'd the honour of it ſome-
what, in my mother's caſe, was, that ſhe
could not heroine it into ſo violent and
hazardous an extream, as one in her
ſituation might have wiſh'd, becauſe the

old

old midwife had really some little claim
to be depended upon,——as much, at least,
as success could give her; having, in the
course of her practice of near twenty
years in the parish, brought every mother's son of them into the world without any one slip or accident which could
fairly be laid to her account.

These facts, tho' they had their weight,
yet did not altogether satisfy some few
scruples and uneasinesses which hung
upon my father's spirits in relation to this
choice.——To say nothing of the natural
workings of humanity and justice,——or of
the yearnings of parental and connubial
love; all which prompted him to leave
as little to hazard as possible in a case of
this kind;——he felt himself concern'd
in a particular manner, that all should
go right in the present case;——from the

ac-

accumulated forrow he lay open to, fhould any evil betide his wife and child in lying-in at *Shandy-Hall.*——He knew the world judged by events, and would add to his afflictions in fuch a misfortune, by loading him with the whole blame of it.——" Alas o'day ;—had Mrs. *Shandy,* " poor gentlewoman! had but her wifh " in going up to town juft to lye-in and " come down again ;—which, they fay, " fhe begg'd and pray'd for upon her " bare knees,——and which, in my opi- " nion, confidering the fortune which " Mr. *Shandy* got with her,—was no fuch " mighty matter to have complied with, " the. lady and her babe might both of " 'em have been alive at this hour."

This exclamation, my father knew was unanfwerable ;—and yet, it was not merely to fhelter himfelf,—nor was

it

it altogether for the care of his offspring
and wife that he feem'd fo extremely
anxious about this point;—my father
had extenfive views of things,————and
ftood, moreover, as he thought, deeply
concern'd in it for the publick good,
from the dread he entertained of the
bad ufes an ill-fated inftance might be
put to.

He was very fenfible that all political
writers upon the fubject had unanimoufly
agreed and lamented, from the beginning of Queen *Elizabeth*'s reign down
to his own time, that the current of men
and money towards the metropolis, upon one frivolous errand or another,—
fet in fo ftrong,—as to become dangerous to our civil rights;—tho', by the
bye,————a *current* was not the image he
took moft delight in,—a *diftemper* was

G 4   here

here his favourite metaphor, and he would run it down into a perfect allego-ry, by maintaining it was identically the fame in the body national as in the body natural, where blood and fpirits were driven up into the head fafter than they could find their ways down ;——a ftop-page of circulation muft enfue, which was death in both cafes.

There was little danger, he would fay, of lofing our liberties by *French* politicks or *French* invafions ;——nor was he fo much in pain of a confumption from the mafs of corrupted matter and ulce-rated humours in our conftitution,—which he hoped was not fo bad as it was imagined ;—but he verily feared, that in fome violent pufh, we fhould go off, all at once, in a ftate-apoplexy ;—and then

then he would fay, *The Lord have mercy upon us all.*

My father was never able to give the hiftory of this diftemper,—without the remedy along with it.

" Was I an abfolute prince, he would fay, pulling up his breeches with both his hands, as he rofe from his arm-chair, " I would appoint able judges, at every " avenue of my metropolis, who fhould " take cognizance of every fool's bufi- " nefs who came there;—and if, upon " a fair and candid hearing, it appeared " not of weight fufficient to leave his " own home, and come up, bag and " baggage, with his wife and children, " farmers fons, *&c. &c.* at his backfide, " they fhould be all fent back, from " conftable to conftable, like vagrants

" as

" as they were, to the place of their le-
" gal settlements. By this means I shall
" take care, that my metropolis totter'd
" not thro' its own weight ;—that the
" head be no longer too big for the bo-
" dy ;—that the extreams, now wasted
" and pin'd in, be restored to their due
" share of nourishment, and regain, with
" it, their natural strength and beauty :—
" I would effectually provide, That the
" meadows and corn-fields, of my do-
" minions, should laugh and sing ;—
" that good chear and hospitality flou-
" rish once more ;—and that such weight
" and influence be put thereby into the
" hands of the Squirality of my king-
" dom, as should counterpoise what I
" perceive my Nobility are now taking
" from them.

" Why

" Why are there fo few palaces and
" gentlemen's feats, he would afk, with
fome emotion, as he walked a-crofs the
room, " throughout fo many delicious
" provinces in *France?* Whence is it that
" the few remaining *Chateaus* amongft
" them are fo difmantled,—fo unfurnifh-
" ed, and in fo ruihous and defolate a
" condition ?—Becaufe, Sir, (he would
fay) " in that kingdom no man has any
" country-intereft to fupport;—the little
" intereft of any kind, which any man
" has any where in it, is concentrated in
" the court, and the looks of the Grand
" Monarch ; by the fun-fhine of whofe
" countenance, or the clouds which pafs
" a-crofs it, every *French* man lives or
" dies."

Another political reafon which prompted my father fo ftrongly to guard againft

the

the leaſt evil accident in my mother's
lying-in in the country,——was, That
any ſuch inſtance would infallibly throw
a balance of power, too great already,
into the weaker veſſels of the gentry, in
his own, or higher ſtations ;——which,
with the many other uſurped rights
which that part of the conſtitution was
hourly eſtabliſhing,——would, in the end,
prove fatal to the monarchical ſyſtem of
domeſtick government eſtabliſhed in the
firſt creation of things by God.

In this point he was entirely of Sir
Robert Filmer's opinion, That the plans
and inſtitutions of the greateſt mo-
narchies in the eaſtern parts of the world,
were, originally, all ſtolen from that ad-
mirable pattern and prototype of this
houſhold and paternal power ;——which,
for a century, he ſaid, and more, had
gra-

gradually been degenerating away into
a mix'd government;——the form of
which, however defirable in great com-
binations of the fpecies,——was very
troublefome in fmall ones,—and feldom
produced any thing, that he faw, but
forrow and confufion.

For all thefe reafons, private and publick, put together,—my father was for
having the man-midwife by all means,—
my mother by no means. My father
begg'd and intreated, fhe would for once
recede from her prerogative in this matter, and fuffer him to choofe for her;—
my mother, on the contrary, infifted upon her privilege in this matter, to choofe
for herfelf,—and have no mortal's help
but the old woman's.——What could my
father do? He was almoft at his wit's
end;——talked it over with her in all
moods;

moods ;—placed his arguments in all
lights ;—argued the matter with her
like a chriſtian,—like a heathen,—like
a huſband,—like a father,—like a pa-
triot,—like a man :—My mother anſwered every thing only like a woman ;
which was a little hard upon her ;—for
as ſhe could not aſſume and fight it out
behind ſuch a variety of characters,—
'twas no fair match ;—'twas ſeven to
one.—What could my mother do ?——
She had the advantage (otherwiſe ſhe
had been certainly overpowered) of a
ſmall reinforcement of chagrine perſonal
at the bottom which bore her up, and
enabled her to diſpute the affair with my
father with ſo equal an advantage,——
that both ſides ſung *Te Deum.* In a
word, my mother was to have the old
woman,—and the operator was to have
licence to drink a bottle of wine with
my

my father and my uncle *Toby Shandy* in the back parlour,—for which he was to be paid five guineas.

I muſt beg leave, before I finiſh this chapter, to enter a caveat in the breaſt of my fair reader ;—and it is this :——— Not to take it abſolutely for granted from an unguarded word or two which I have dropp'd in it,———" That I am a married man."—I own the tender appellation of my dear, dear *Jenny*,—with ſome other ſtrokes of conjugal knowledge, interſperſed here and there, might, naturally enough, have miſled the moſt candid judge in the world into ſuch a determination againſt me.—All I plead for, in this caſe, Madam, is ſtriƈt juſtice, and that you do ſo much of it, to me as well as to yourſelf,—as not to prejudge or receive ſuch an impreſſion of me, till

you

you have better evidence, than I am
pofitive, at prefent, can be produced
againft me :—Not that I can be fo vain
or unreafonable, Madam, as to defire
you fhould therefore think, that my dear,
dear *Jenny* is my kept miftrefs ;—no,—
that would be flattering my character in
the other extream, and giving it an air
of freedom, which, perhaps, it has no
kind of right to.   All I contend for, is
the utter impoffibility for fome volumes,
that you, or the moft penetrating fpirit
upon earth, fhould know how this matter really ftands.—It is not impoffible,
but that my dear, dear *Jenny!* tender as
the appellation is, may be my child.——
Confider,—I was born in the year eighteen.—Nor is there any thing unnatural
or extravagant in the fuppofition, that
my dear *Jenny* may be my friend.——
Friend!—My friend.—Surely, Madam,

a friendſhip between the two ſexes may
ſubſiſt, and be ſupported without——
Fy ! Mr. *Shandy* :—Without any thing,
Madam, but that tender and delicious
ſentiment, which ever mixes in friendſhip, where there is a difference of ſex.
Let me intreat you to ſtudy the pure
and ſentimental parts of the beſt *French*
Romances ;——it will really, Madam,
aſtoniſh you to ſee with what a variety
of chaſte expreſſion this delicious ſentiment, which I have the honour to ſpeak
of, is dreſs'd out.

C H A P. XIX.

I Would ſooner undertake to explain
the hardeſt problem in Geometry,
than pretend to account for it, that a
gentleman of my father's great good

, VOL. I.   H   ſenſe,

fenfe,——knowing, as the reader muft.
have obferved him, and curious too, in
philofophy,——wife alfo in political reafoning,——and in polemical (as he will
find) no way ignorant,——could be capable of entertaining a notion in his head,
fo out of the common track,——that I fear
the reader, when I come to mention it to
him, if he is the leaft of a cholerick temper, will immediately throw the book by;
if mercurial, he will laugh moft heartily
at it;——and if he is of a grave and fa-
turnine caft, he will, at firft fight, abfolutely condemn as fanciful and extravagant; and that was in refpect to the
choice and impofition of Chriftian names,
on which he thought a great deal more
depended than what fuperficial minds
were capable of conceiving.

His

His opinion, in this matter, was, That there was a ſtrange kind of magick bias, which good or bad names, as he called them, irreſiſtibly impreſs'd upon our characters and conduct.

The Hero of *Cervantes* argued not the point with more ſeriouſneſs,——nor had he more faith,——or more to ſay on the powers of Necromancy in diſhonouring his deeds,—or on Dulcinea's name, in ſhedding luſtre upon them, than my father had on thoſe of Trismegistus or Archimedes, on the one hand,—or of Nyky and Simkin on the other. How many Cæsars and Pompeys, he would ſay, by mere inſpiration of the names, have been render'd worthy of them? And how many, he would add, are there who might have done exceeding well in the world, had not their characters and

H 2   ſpirits

spirits been totally deprefs'd and Nico-
demus'd into nothing.

  . . I see plainly, Sir, by your looks, (or
as the cafe happen'd) my father would
fay,—that you do not heartily fubfcribe
to this opinion of mine,—which, to thofe,
he would add, who have not carefully
fifted it to the bottom,—I own has an
air more of fancy than of folid reafoning
in it;——and yet, my dear Sir, if I may
prefume to know your character, I am
morally affured, I fhould hazard little in
ftating a cafe to you,—not as a party in
the difpute,—but as a judge, and truft-
ing my appeal upon it to your own good
fenfe and candid difquifition in this matter;——you are a perfon free from as
many narrow prejudices of education as
moft men;—and, if I may prefume to
penetrate further into you,—of a libe-

  . 3   rality

rality of genius above bearing down an opinion, merely becaufe it wants friends. Your fon!—your dear fon,—from whofe fweet and open temper you have fo much to expect.—Your BILLY, Sir!—would you, for the world, have called him JUDAS?—Would you, my dear Sir, he would fay, laying his hand upon your breaft, with the genteeleft addrefs,—and in that foft and irrefiftible *piano* of voice, which the nature of the *argumentum ad hominem* abfolutely requires,—Would you, Sir, if a *Jew* of a godfather had propofed the name for your child, and offered you his purfe along with it, would you have confented to fuch a defecration of him?——O my God! he would fay, looking up, if I know your temper right, Sir,—you are incapable of it;——you would have trampled upon the offer;—

you

you would have thrown the temptation at the tempter's head with abhorrence.

Your greatnefs of mind in this action, which I admire, with that generous contempt of money which you fhew me in the whole tranfaction, is really noble;—and what renders it more fo, is the principle of it;—the workings of a parent's love upon the truth and conviction of this very hypothefis, namely, That was your fon called JUDAS,—the fordid and treacherous idea, fo infeparable from the name, would have accompanied him thro' life like his fhadow, and, in the end, made a mifer and a rafcal of him, in fpight, Sir, of your example.

I never knew a man able to anfwer this argument.——But, indeed, to fpeak of my father as he was;—he was certainly
tainly

tainly irrefiftible, both in his orations and
difputations ;—he was born an orator;—
Θεοδίδακῖ@·.—Perfuafion hung upon his
lips, and the elements of Logick and
Rhetorick were fo blended up in him,—
and, withall, he had fo fhrewd guefs at
the weakneffes and paffions of his re-
fpondent,———that NATURE might have
ftood up and faid,—" This man is elo-
quent." In fhort, whether he was on
the weak or the ftrong fide of the queftion, 'twas hazardous in either cafe to
attack him :—And yet, 'tis ftrange, he
had never read *Cicero* nor *Quintilian de
Oratore*, nor *Ifocrates*, nor *Ariftotle*, nor
Longinus amongft the antients ;———nor
Voffius, nor *Skioppius*, nor *Ramus*, nor
Farnaby amongft the moderns ;—and
what is more aftonifhing, he had never in
his whole life the leaft light or fpark of
fubtilty ftruck into his mind, by one fingle

H 4 lecture

lecture upon *Crackenthorp* or *Burgerfdi-*
cius, or any *Dutch* logician or commenta-
tor ;—he knew not fo much as in what
the difference of an argument *ad igno-*
rantiam, and an argument *ad hominem*
confifted; fo that I well remember, when
he went up along with me to enter my
name at *Jefus College* in ****,—it was
a matter of juft wonder with my worthy
tutor, and two or three fellows of that
learned fociety,—that a man who knew
not fo much as the names of his tools,
fhould be able to work after that fafhion
with 'em.

To work with them in the beft manner he could, was what my father was,
however, perpetually forced upon ;——
for he had a thoufand little fceptical notions of the comick kind to defend,——
moft of which notions, I verily believe,

at

at firſt enter'd upon the footing of mere
whims, and of a *vive la Bagatelle* ; and as
ſuch he would make merry with them for
half an hour or ſo, and having ſharpen'd
his wit upon 'em, diſmiſs them till another day.

I mention this, not only as matter of
hypotheſis or conjecture upon the progreſs and eſtabliſhment of my father's
many odd opinions,—but as a warning to
the learned reader againſt the indiſcreet
reception of ſuch gueſts, who, after a
free and undiſturbed enterance, for ſome
years, into our brains,—at length claim
a kind of ſettlement there,——working
ſometimes like yeaſt ;—but more generally after the manner of the gentle paſ-
ſion, beginning in jeſt,—but ending in
downright earneſt.

Whether

Whether this was the cafe of the fingularity of my father's notions,—or that
his judgment, at length, became the
dupe of his wit;—or how far, in many
of his notions, he might, tho' odd, be
abfolutely right;——the reader, as he
comes at them, fhall decide. All that
I maintain here, is, that in this one, of
the influence of Chriftian names, however it gain'd footing, he was ferious;—
he was all uniformity;—he was fyftema-
tical, and, like all fyftematick reafoners,
he would move both heaven and earth,
and twift and torture every thing in nature to fupport his hypothefis. In a
word, I repeat it over again;—he was
ferious;—and, in confequence of it, he
would lofe all kind of patience whenever
he faw people, efpecially of condition,
who fhould have known better,——as
carelefs and as indifferent about the name
they

they impofed upon their child,—or more
fo, than in the choice of *Ponto* or *Cupid*
for their puppy dog.

This, he would fay, look'd ill ;—and
had, moreover, this particular aggrava-
tion in it, *viz.* That when once a vile
name was wrongfully or injudicioufly
given, 'twas not like the cafe of a man's
character, which, when wrong'd, might
hereafter be clear'd ;——and, poffibly,
fometime or other, if not in the man's life,
at leaft after his death,—be, fomehow
or other, fet to rights with the world :
But the injury of this, he would fay,
could never be undone ;—nay, he doubt-
ed even whether an act of parliament
could reach it :——He knew as well as
you, that the legiflature affum'd a power
over furnames ;—but for very ftrong
reafons, which he could give, it had ne-

ver

ver yet adventured, he would fay, to go
a ftep further.

It was obfervable, that tho' my father,
in confequence of this opinion, had, as I
have told you, the ftrongeft likings and
diflikings towards certain names;—that
there were ftill numbers of names which
hung fo equally in the balance before
him, that they were abfolutely indifferent
to him. *Jack*, *Dick*, and *Tom* were of
this clafs: Thefe my father call'd neutral
names;—affirming of them, without a
fatyr, That there had been as many
knaves and fools, at leaft, as wife and
good men, fince the world began, who
had indifferently borne them;—fo that,
like equal forces acting againft each other
in contrary directions, he thought they
mutually deftroyed each others effects;
for which reafon, he would often declare,
He,

He would not give a cherry-ſtone to
chooſe amongſt them. *Bob*, which was
my brother's name, was another of theſe
neutral kinds of Chriſtian names, which
operated very little either way ; and as
my father happen'd to be at *Epſom*, when
it was given him,—he would oft times
thank heaven it was no worſe. *Andrew*
was ſomething like a negative quantity
in Algebra with him ;—'twas worſe, he
ſaid, than nothing.—*William* ſtood pretty high :——*Numps* again was low with
him ;—and *Nick*, he ſaid, was the DEVIL.

But, of all the names in the univerſe,
he had the moſt unconquerable averſion
for TRISTRAM ;—he had the loweſt and
moſt contemptible opinion of it of any
thing in the world,—thinking it could
poſſibly produce nothing in *rerum naturâ*,
but what was extreamly mean and pitiful :

ful: So that in the midſt of a diſpute on the ſubject, in which, by the bye, he was frequently involved,——he would ſometimes break off in a ſudden and ſpi- rited EPIPHONEMA, or rather EROTESIS, raiſed a third, and ſometimes a full fifth, above the key of the diſcourſe,——and demand it categorically of his antagoniſt, Whether he would take upon him to ſay, he had ever remember'd,——whether he had ever read,—or even whether he had ever heard tell of a man, call'd *Triſtram*, performing any thing great or worth re- cording ?—No—, he would ſay,—TRI- STRAM !—The thing is impoſſible.

What could be wanting in my father but to have wrote a book to publiſh this notion of his to the world ? Little boots it to the ſubtle ſpeculatiſt to ſtand ſingle in his opinions,—unleſs he gives them

proper

proper vent :—It was the identical thing
which my father did ;—for in the year
fixteen, which was two years before I was
born, he was at the pains of writing an
exprefs Dissertation fimply upon the
word *Triſtram*,—ſhewing the world, with
great candour and modeſty, the grounds
of his great abhorrence to the name.

When this ſtory is compared with the
title-page,—Will not the gentle reader
pity my father from his foul?—to fee an
orderly and well-difpofed gentleman, who
tho' fingular,—yet inoffenfive in his notions,—ſo played upon in them by crofs
purpofes;——to look down upon the
ſtage, and fee him baffled and over-
thrown in all his little fyftems and wifhes;
to behold a train of events perpetually
falling out againſt him, and in fo critical
and cruel a way, as if they had purpofed-

6   ly

ly been plann'd and pointed againſt him, merely to inſult his ſpeculations.——In a word, to behold ſuch a one, in his old age, ill-fitted for troubles, ten times in a day ſuffering ſorrow;—ten times in a day calling the child of his prayers TRI-STRAM!——Melancholy diſſyllable of found! which, to his ears, was uniſon to *Nicompoop*, and every name vitupera-tive under heaven.——By his aſhes! I ſwear it,—if ever malignant ſpirit took pleaſure, or buſied itſelf in traverſing the purpoſes of mortal man,—it muſt have been here;—and if it was not neceſſary I ſhould be born before I was chriſtened, I would this moment give the reader an account of it.

CHAP.

C H A P. XX.

————How could you, Madam, be
fo inattentive in reading the laſt chapter?
I told you in it, *That my mother was not a*
papiſt.——Papiſt! You told me no ſuch
thing, Sir. Madam, I beg leave to repeat it over again, That I told you as
plain, at leaſt, as words, by direct inference, could tell you ſuch a thing.—Then,
Sir, I muſt have miſs'd a page.——No, Madam,—you have not miſs'd a word.———
Then I was aſleep, Sir.—My pride, Madam, cannot allow you that refuge.———
Then, I declare, I know nothing at all
about the matter.——That, Madam, is the
very fault I lay to your charge; and as
a puniſhment for it, I do inſiſt upon it,
that you immediately turn back, that is,
as ſoon as you get to the next full ſtop,
and read the whole chapter over again.

I have impofed this penance upon the lady, neither out of wantonnefs or cruelty, but from the beft of motives ; and there-fore fhall make her no apology for it when fhe returns back :—'Tis to rebuke a vicious tafte which has crept into thou-fands befides herfelf,—of reading ftraight forwards, more in queft of the adven-tures, than of the deep erudition and knowledge which a book of this caft, if read over as it fhould be, would infalli-bly impart with them.——The mind fhould be accuftomed to make wife re-flections, and draw curious conclufions as it goes along ; the habitude of which made *Pliny* the younger affirm, " That he never read a book fo bad, but he drew fome profit from it." The ftories of *Greece* and *Rome*, run over without this turn and application,—do lefs fervice, I affirm it, than the hiftory of *Parifmus* and

Par-

Parifmenus, or of the Seven Champions
of *England,* read with it.

————But here comes my fair Lady.
Have you read over again the chapter,
Madam, as I defired you ?—You have :
And did you not obferve the paffage,
upon the fecond reading, which admits
the inference ?——Not a word like it !
Then, Madam, be pleafed to ponder well
the laft line but one of the chapter, where
I take upon me to fay, " It was *neceffary*
I fhould be born before I was chriften'd."
Had my mother, Madam, been a Papift,
that confequence did not follow *.

I 2 It

* The *Romifh* Rituals direct the baptizing of the
child, in cafes of danger, *before* it is born ;—but
upon this provifo, That fome part or other of the
child's body be feen by the baptizer :——But the
Doctors of the *Sorbonne,* by a deliberation held
amongft them, *April* 10, 1733,—have enlarged the
powers

It is a terrible misfortune for this same book of mine, but more so to the Republick of Letters ;—so that my own is quite swallowed up in the consideration of it,—that this self-same vile pruriency for fresh adventures in all things, has got so strongly into our habit and humours,—and so wholly intent are we upon satisfying the impatience of our concupiscence that way,—that nothing but

powers of the midwives, by determining, That tho' no part of the child's body should appear,—— that baptism shall, nevertheless, be administered to it by injection,—*par le moyen d' une petite Canulle.*— *Anglicè a squirt.*—'Tis very strange that St. *Thomas Aquinas,* who had so good a mechanical head, both for tying and untying the knots of school divinity,—should, after so much pains bestowed upon this,—give up the point at last, as a second *La chose impossible,*—" Infantes in maternis uteris existentes (quoth St. *Thomas*) baptizari possunt *nullo modo.*"— O *Thomas ! Thomas !*

If

but the grofs and more carnal parts of a compofition will go down :—The fubtle hints and fly communications of fcience fly off, like fpirits, upwards ;———the heavy moral efcapes downwards ; and both the one and the other are as much loft to the world, as if they were ftill left in the bottom of the ink-horn.

I wifh the male-reader has not pafs'd by many a one, as quaint and curious as this one, in which the female-reader has been detected. I wifh it may have its effects;—and that all good people, both male and female, from her example, may be taught to think as well as read.

I 3   ME-

If the reader has the curiofity to fee the queftion upon baptifm, *by injection*, as prefented to the Doctors of the *Sorbonne*,—with their confultation thereupon, it is as follows.

MEMOIRE preſenté à Meſſieurs les Docteurs de SORBONNE *.

*U*N *Chirurgien Accoucheur, repreſente à Meſſieurs les Docteurs de Sorbonne, qu' il y a des cas, quoique très rares, où une mere ne ſçauroit accoucher, & même où l'enfant eſt tellement renfermé dans le ſein de ſa mere, qu' il ne fait parbitre aucune partie de ſon corps, ce qui ſeroit un cas, ſui-vant les Rituels, de lui conférer, du moins ſous condition, le baptême. Le Chirurgien, qui conſulte, prétend, par le moyen d'une petite canulle, de pouvoir baptiſer imme-diatement l'enfant, ſans faire aucun tort à la mere.——Il demand ſi ce moyen, qu' il vient de propoſer, eſt permis & légitime, et s'il peut s'en ſervir dans le cas qu' il vient d'expoſer.*

RE-

* Vide Deventer. Paris Edit. 4to, 1734. p. 366.

REPONSE

LE Conseil estime, que la question proposée souffre de grandes difficultes. Les Théologiens posent d'un coté pour principe, que le baptéme, qui est une naissance spirituelle, suppose une premiere naissance ; il faut être né dans le monde, pour renaître en Jesus Christ, comme ils l'enseignent. S. Thomas, 3 part. quæst. 88. artic. 11. suit cette doctrine comme une verité constante ; l'on ne peut, dit ce S. Docteur, baptiser les enfans qui sont renfermés dans le sein de leurs Meres, et S. Thomas est fondé sur ce, que les enfans ne sont point nés, & ne peuvent être comptés parmi les autres hommes ; d'ou il conclud, qu'ils ne peuvent être l'objet d'une action extérieure, pour recevoir par leur ministére, les sacremens nécessaires au salut : Pueri in maternis uteris existentes nondum pro-

dierunt

dierant in lucem ut cum aliis hominibus
vitam ducant ; unde non poffunt fubjici
actioni humanæ, ut per eorum minifte-
rium facramenta recipiant ad falutem.
*Les rituels ordonnent dans la pratique ce que
les théologiens ont établi fur les mêmes ma-
tiéres, & ils deffendent tous d'une maniére
uniforme de baptifer les enfans qui font renfermés dans le fein de leurs meres, s'ils ne
font paroitre quelque partie de leurs corps.
Le concours des théologiens, & des rituels,
qui font les régles des diocéfes, parôit former
une autorité qui termine la queftion prefente ;
cependant le confeil de confcience confiderant
d'un coté, que le raifonnement des théologiens
eft uniquement fondé fur une raifon de con-
venance, & que la deffenfe des rituels, fuppofe
que l'on ne peut baptifer immediatement les
enfans ainfi renfermés dans le fein de leurs
meres, ce qui eft contre la fuppofition prefente ;
& d'un autre côté, confiderant que les mêmes*

théo-

théologiens enseignent, que l'on peut risquer les sacremens qu' Jesus Christ a établis comme des moyens faciles, mais nécessaires pour sanctifier les hommes ; & d'ailleurs estimant, que les enfans renfermés dans le sein de leurs meres, pourroient être capables de salut; parce qu'ils sont capables de damnation ;— pour ces considerations, & eu égard a l'exposé, suivant lequel on assure avoir trouvé un moyen certain de baptiser ces enfans ainsi renfermés, sans faire aucun tort à la mere, le Conseil estime que l'on pourroit se servir du moyen proposé, dans la confiance qu'il a, que Dieu n' a point laissé ces sortes d'enfans sans aucuns secours, & supposant, comme il est exposé, que le moyen dont il s'agit est propre à leur procurer le baptême ; cependant comme il s'agiroit, en autorisant la pratique proposée, de changer une régle universellement établie, le Conseil croit que celui qui consulte doit s'addresser a son évêque, & à qui il ap-

partient

partient de juger de l'utilité, & du danger
du moyen proposé, & comme, sous le bon
plaisir de l'evêque, le conseil estime qu'il fau-
droit recourir au Pape, qui a le droit d'ex-
pliquer les régles de l'eglise, et d' y déroger
dans le cas, ou la loi ne sçauroit obliger, quelque sage & quelque utile que paroisse la maniére
de baptiser dont il s'agit, le conseil ne pourroit
l'approuver sans le concours de ces deux auto-
rités. On conseile au moins à celui qui consulte,
de s'addresser à son evêque, & de lui faire part
de la presente décision, afin que, si le prelat
entre dans les raisons sur lesquelles les docteurs
soussignés s'appuyent, il puisse être autorisé dans
le cas de nécessité, ou il risqueroit trop d'at-
tendre que la permission fût demandée & ac-
cordée d'employer le moyen qu' il propose si
avantageux au salut de l'enfant. Au reste
le conseil, en estimant que l'on pourroit s'en
servir croit cependant, que si les enfans dont
il s'agit, venoient au monde, contre l'esperance
de

*de ceux qui se feroient servis du même moyen,
il seroit nécessaire de les baptiser sous condition, & en cela le conseil se conforme à tous
les rituels, qui en autorisant le baptême d'un
enfant qui fait paroître quelque partie de son
corps, enjoignent néantmoins, & ordonnent de
le baptiser sous condition, s'il vient heu-
reusement au monde.*

Déliberé en *Sorbonne*, le 10 *Avril*, 1733.

A. Le Moyne,
L. De Romigny,
De Marcilly.

Mr. *Tristram Shandy*'s compliments to
Messrs. *Le Moyne, De Romigny*, and *De
Marcilly*, hopes they all rested well the
night after so tiresome a consultation.——
He begs to know, whether, after the ceremony of marriage, and before that of
con-

confummation, the baptizing all the Ho-
munculi at once, flap-dafh, by *injection*,
would not be a fhorter and fafer cut ftill;
on condition, as above, That if the Ho-
munculi do well and come fafe into the
world after this, That each and every of
them fhall be baptized again (*fous condition.*)——And provided, in the fecond
place, That the thing can be done,
which Mr. *Shandy* apprehends it may,
par le moyen d'une petite canulle, and
fans faire aucun tort au pere.

C H A P. XXI.

——I wonder what's all that noife,
and running backwards and forwards
for, above ftairs, quoth my father, ad-
drefling himfelf, after an hour and a
half's filence, to my uncle *Toby*,——who

you

you muſt know, was ſitting on the oppoſite ſide of the fire, ſmoking his ſocial
pipe all the time, in mute contemplation
of a new pair of black-pluſh-breeches
which he had got on;—What can they
be doing brother? quoth my father,—
we can ſcarce hear ourſelves talk.

I think, replied my uncle *Toby*, taking
his pipe from his mouth, and ſtriking
the head of it two or three times upon
the nail of his left thumb, as he began
his ſentence,——I think, ſays he:——
But to enter rightly into my uncle *Toby*'s
ſentiments upon this matter, you muſt
be made to enter firſt a little into his
character, the out-lines of which I ſhall
juſt give you, and then the dialogue between him and my father will go on as
well again.

—Pray

—Pray what was that man's name,—
for I write in such a hurry, I have no
time to recollect or look for it,——who
first made the observation, " That there
was great inconstancy in our air and climate?" Whoever he was, 'twas a just
and good observation in him.—But the
corollary drawn from it, namely, " That
it is this which has furnished us with
such a variety of odd and whimsical characters;"—that was not his;—it was
found out by another man, at least a
century and a half after him :—Then
again,—that this copious store-house of
original materials, is the true and natural
cause that our Comedies are so much better than those of *France*, or any others that
either have, or can be wrote upon the
Continent;——that discovery was not
fully made till about the middle of king
William's reign,—when the great *Dryden*,

in

in writing one of his long prefaces, (if I
miftake not) moft fortunately hit upon
it. Indeed towards the latter end of
queen *Anne*, the great *Addifon* began to
patronize the notion, and more fully ex-
plained it to the world in one or two of
his Spectators;—but the difcovery was
not his.—Then, fourthly and laftly, that
this ftrange irregularity in our climate,
producing fo ftrange an irregularity in
our characters,——doth thereby, in
fome fort, make us amends, by giving
us fomewhat to make us merry with when
the weather will not fuffer us to go out
of doors,—that obfervation is my own;—
and was ftruck out by me this very rainy
day, *March* 26, 1759, and betwixt the
hours of nine and ten in the morning.

Thus,—thus my fellow labourers and
affociates in this great harveft of our
learning,

learning, now ripening before our eyes;
thus it is, by flow fteps of cafual increafe,
that our knowledge phyfical, metaphy-
fical, phyfiological, polemical, nautical,
mathematical, ænigmatical, technical,
biographical, romantical, chemical, and
obftetrical, with fifty other branches of it,
(moft of 'em ending, as thefe do, in *ical*)
have, for thefe two laft centuries and
more, gradually been creeping upwards
towards that Ακμὴ of their perfections,
from which, if we may form a conjecture
from the advances of thefe laft feven
years, we cannot poffibly be far off.

When that happens, it is to be hoped,
it will put an end to all kind of writings
whatfoever ;—the want of all kind of
writing will put an end to all kind of
reading ;—and that in time, *As war be-
gets poverty, poverty peace,*——muft, in
course,

courfe, put an end to all kind of know ledge,—and then——we fhall have all to begin over again ; or, in other words, be exactly where we ftarted.

———Happy! thrice happy Times! I only wifh that the æra of my begetting, as well as the mode and manner of it, had been a little alter'd,—or that it could have been put off with any convenience to my father or mother, for fome twenty or five-and-twenty years longer, when a man in the literary world might have ftood fome chance.———

But I forget my uncle *Toby*, whom all this while we have left knocking the afhes out of his tobacco pipe.

His humour was of that particular fpecies, which does honour to our atmo-

ſphere; and I ſhould have made no ſcru-
ple of ranking him amongſt one of the
firſt-rate productions of it, had not there
appear'd too many ſtrong lines in it of a
family-likeneſs, which ſhewed that he
derived the ſingularity of his temper
more from blood, than either wind or
water, or any modifications or combina-
tions of them whatever: And I have,
therefore, oft times wondered, that my
father, tho' I believe he had his reaſons
for it, upon his obſerving ſome tokens
of excentricity in my courſe when I was
a boy,—ſhould never once endeavour to
account for them in this way; for all the
SHANDY FAMILY were of an original
character throughout;——I mean the
males,—the females had no character at
all,—except, indeed, my great aunt DI-
NAH, who, about ſixty years ago, was
married and got with child by the coachman,

man, for which my father, according to his hypothefis of Chriftian names, would often fay, She might thank her godfathers and godmothers.

It will feem very ftrange,——and I would as foon think of dropping a riddle in the reader's way, which is not my intereft to do, as fet him upon gueffing how it could come to pafs, that an event of this kind, fo many years after it had happened, fhould be referved for the interruption of the peace and unity, which otherwife fo cordially fubfifted, between my father and my uncle *Toby*. One would have thought, that the whole force of the misfortune fhould have fpent and wafted itfelf in the family at firft,—as is generally the cafe :—But nothing ever wrought with our family after the ordinary way. Poffibly at the

K 2   very

very time this happened, it might have
fomething elfe to afflict it; and as afflictions are fent down for our good, and
that as this had never done the SHANDY
FAMILY any good at all, it might lye
waiting till apt times and circumftances
fhould give it an opportunity to difcharge
its office.————Obferve, I determine
nothing upon this.————My way is
ever to point out to the curious, different tracts of inveftigation, to come at
the firft fprings of the events I tell ;—
not with a pedantic *Fefcue*,—or in the
decifive Manner of *Tacitus*, who outwits
himfelf and his reader ;—but with the
officious humility of a heart devoted to
the affiftance merely of the inquifitive ;—
to them I write,————and by them I fhall
be read,————if any fuch reading as this
could be fuppofed to hold out fo long,
to the very end of the world.

Why

Why this caufe of forrow, therefore,
was thus referved for my father and uncle, is undetermined by me. But how
and in what direction it exerted itfelf, fo
as to become the caufe of diffatisfaction
between them, after it began to operate,
is what I am able to explain with great
exactnefs, and is as follows :

My uncle TOBY SHANDY, Madam,
was a gentleman, who, with the virtues
which ufually conftitute the character of
a man of honour and rectitude,—poffef-
fed one in a very eminent degree, which
is feldom or never put into the catalogue;
and that was a moft extream and unparallel'd modefty of nature ;——tho' I
correct the word nature, for this reafon,
that I may not prejudge a point which
muft fhortly come to a hearing; and that
is, Whether this modefty of his was na-

tural

túral or acquir'd. ———— Which ever
way my uncle *Toby* came by it, 'twas
neverthelefs modefty in the trueft fenfe
of it; and that is, Madam, not in regard
to words, for he was fo unhappy as to
have very little choice in them,—but to
things;———and this kind of modefty fo
poffefs'd him, and it arofe to fuch a
height in him, as almoft to equal, if
. fuch a thing could be, even the modefty
of a woman: That female nicety, Madam, and inward cleanlinefs of mind and
fancy, in your fex, which makes you fo
much the awe of ours.

You will imagine, Madam, that my
uncle *Toby* had contracted all this from
this very fource;—that he had fpent a
great part of his time in converfe with
your fex; and that, from a thorough
knowledge of you, and the force of imita-
tion

tion which such fair examples render ir-
resistable,——he had acquired this amiable
turn of mind.

I wish I could say so,——for unless it
was with his sister-in-law, my father's
wife and my mother,——my uncle *Toby*
scarce exchanged three words with the
sex in as many years ;——no, he got it,
Madam, by a blow.——A blow !——Yes,
Madam, it was owing to a blow from a
stone, broke off by a ball from the para-
pet of a horn-work at the siege of *Namur*,
which struck full upon my uncle *Toby*'s
groin.——Which way could that effect it ?
The story of that, Madam, is long and
interesting ;——but it would be running
my history all upon heaps to give it you
here.——'Tis for an episode hereafter ;
and every circumstance relating to it in
its proper place, shall be faithfully laid

before

before you :——'Till then, it is not in my
power to give further light into this
matter, or say more than what I have
said already,——That my uncle *Toby* was
a gentleman of unparallel'd modesty,
which happening to be somewhat sub-
tilized and rarified by the constant heat
of a little family-pride,——they both so
wrought together within him, that he
could never bear to hear the affair of my
aunt DINAH touch'd upon, but with the
greatest emotion.——The least hint of it
was enough to make the blood fly into
his face;—but when my father enlarged
upon the story in mixed companies,
which the illustration of his hypothesis
frequently obliged him to do,—the un-
fortunate blight of one of the fairest
branches of the family, would set my
uncle *Toby*'s honour and modesty a'bleed-
ing; and he would often take my father

ther aside, in the greateſt concern imaginable, to expoſtulate and tell him, he
would give him any thing in the world,
only to let the ſtory reſt.

My father, I believe, had the trueſt
love and tenderneſs for my uncle *Toby*,
that ever one brother bore towards another, and would have done any thing in
nature, which one brother in reaſon could
have deſir'd of another, to have made my
uncle *Toby*'s heart eaſy in this, or any o-
ther point. But this lay out of his power.

———My father, as I told you, was a
philoſopher in grain, — ſpeculative, —
ſyſtematical ;—and my aunt *Dinah*'s affair was a matter of as much conſequence
to him, as the retrogradation of the planets to *Copernicus* :—The backſlidings of
Venus in her orbit fortified the *Copernican*
ſyſtem

fyftem, call'd fo after his name; and the backflidings of my aunt Dinah in her orbit, did the fame fervice in eftablifhing my father's fyftem, which, I truft, will for ever hereafter be call'd the *Shandean Syftem*, after his.

In any other family difhonour, my father, I believe, had as nice a fenfe of fhame as any man whatever;——and neither he, nor, I dare fay, *Copernicus*, would have divulged the affair in either cafe, or have taken the leaft notice of it to the world, but for the obligations they owed, as they thought, to truth.—— *Amicus Plato*, my father would fay, conftruing the words to my uncle *Toby*, as he went along, *Amicus Plato*; that is, DINAH was my aunt;—*fed magis amica veritas*——but TRUTH is my fifter.

This

This contrariety of humours betwixt my father and my uncle, was the fource of many a fraternal fquabble. The one could not bear to hear the tale of family difgrace recorded,————and the other would fcarce ever let a day pafs to an end without fome hint at it.

For God's fake, my uncle *Toby* would cry,————and for my fake, and for all our fakes, my dear brother *Shandy*,——do let this ftory of our aunt's and her afhes fleep in peace ;————how can you,————— how can you have fo little feeling and compaffion for the character of our fa-mily :————What is the character of a fa-mily to an hypothefis ? my father would reply.————Nay, if you come to that— what is the life of a family :————The life of a family !——my uncle *Toby* would fay, throwing himfelf back in his arm-

chair

chair, and lifting up his hands, his eyes, and one leg.———Yes the life,———my father would fay, maintaining his point. How many thoufands of 'em are there every year that comes caft away, (in all civilized countries at leaft)———and confider'd as nothing but common air, in competition of an hypothefis. In my plain fenfe of things, my uncle *Toby*, would anfwer,———every fuch inftance is downright MURDER, let who will commit it.———There lies your miftake, my father would reply;———for, in *Foro Scientiæ* there is no fuch thing as MUR-DER,———'tis only DEATH, brother.

My uncle *Toby* would never offer to anfwer this by any other kind of argument, than that of whiftling half a dozen bars of *Lillabullero*.———You muft know

it

it was the ufual channel thro' which his paffions got vent, when any thing fhocked or furprifed him ;——but efpecially when any thing, which he deem'd very abfurd, was offered.

As not one of our logical writers, nor any of the commentators upon them, that I remember, have thought proper to give a name to this particular fpecies of argument,—I here take the liberty to do it myfelf, for two reafons. Firft, That, in order to prevent all confufion in difputes, it may ftand as much diftinguifhed for ever, from every other fpecies of argument,————as the *Argumentum ad Verecundiam*, *ex Abfurdo*, *ex Fortiori*, or any other argument whatfoever :————And, fecondly, That it may be faid by my children's children, when my head is laid to reft,————that their learned grand- father's

5   head

head had been bufied to as much purpofe once, as other people's :—That he
had invented a name,—and generoufly
thrown it into the TREASURY of the
Ars Logica, for one of the moft unanfwerable arguments in the whole fcience.
And if the end of difputation is more to
filence than convince,—they may add, if
they pleafe, to one of the beft arguments
too.

I do therefore, by thefe prefents,
ftrictly order and command, That it be
known and diftinguifhed by the name
and title of the *Argumentum Fiftulatorium,*
and no other;—and that it rank hereafter with the *Argumentum Baculinum,* and
the *Argumentum ad Crumenam,* and for
ever hereafter be treated of in the fame
chapter.

As

As for the *Argumentum Tripodium*, which
is never ufed but by the woman againft
the man ;—and the *Argumentum ad Rem*,
which, contrarywife, is made ufe of by
the man only againft the woman :—As
thefe two are enough in confcience for
one lecture ;——and, moreover, as the
one is the beft anfwer to the other,—let
them likewife be kept apart, and be
treated of in a place by themfelves.

C H A P. XXII.

THE learned Bifhop *Hall*, I mean
the famous Dr. *Jofeph Hall*, who
was Bifhop of *Exeter* in King *James* the
Firft's reign, tells us in one of his *Decads*,
at the end of his divine art of meditation,
imprinted at *London*, in the year 1610,
by *John Beal*, dwelling in *Alderfgate-ftreet*,

" That

" That it is an abominable thing for a man to commend himfelf;"—and I really think it is fo.

And yet, on the other hand, when a thing is executed in a mafterly kind of a fafhion, which thing is not likely to be found out;—I think it is full as abominable, that a man fhould lofe the honour of it, and go out of the world with the conceit of it rotting in his head.

This is precifely my fituation.

For in this long digreffion which I was accidentally led into, as in all my digreffions (one only excepted) there is a mafter-ftroke of digreffive fkill, the merit of which has all along, I fear, been overlooked by my reader,—not for want of penetration in him,—but becaufe 'tis

an

an excellence feldom looked for, or ex-
pected indeed, in a digreffion ;—and it
is this : That tho' my digreffions are all
fair, as you obferve,—and that I fly off
from what I am about, as far and as often too as any writer in *Great-Britain* ;
yet I conftantly take care to order affairs
fo, that my main bufinefs does not ftand
ftill in my abfence.

I was juft going, for example, to have
given you the great out-lines of my uncle
Toby's moft whimfical character ;—when
my aunt *Dinah* and the coachman came
a-crofs us, and led us a vagary fome mil-
lions of miles into the very heart of the
planetary fyftem : Notwithftanding all
this you perceive that the drawing of
my uncle *Toby*'s character went on gently
all the time ;—not the great contours of
it,—that was impoffible,—but fome fa-

miliar ftrokes and faint defignations of it, were here and there touch'd in, as we went along, fo that you are much better acquainted with my uncle *Toby* now than you was before.

By this contrivance the machinery of my work is of a fpecies by itfelf; two contrary motions are introduced into it, and reconciled, which were thought to be at variance with each other. In a word, my work is digreffive, and it is progreffive too,—and at the fame time.

This, Sir, is a very different ftory from that of the earth's moving round her axis, in her diurnal rotation, with her progrefs in her elliptick orbit which brings about the year, and conftitutes that variety and viciffitude of feafons we enjoy ;—though I own it fuggefted the
thought,

thought,——as I believe the greateſt of our boaſted improvements and diſcoveries have come from ſome ſuch trifling hints. .

Digreſſions, inconteſtably, are the ſunſhine;——they are the life, the ſoul of reading;——take them out of this book for inſtance,——you might as well take the book along with them;——one cold eternal winter would reign in every page of it; reſtore them to the writer;——he ſteps forth like a bridegroom,——bids All hail; brings in variety, and forbids the appetite to fail.

All the dexterity is in the good cookery and management of them, ſo as to be not only for the advantage of the reader, but alſo of the author, whoſe diſtreſs, in this matter, is truely pitiable :

For

For, if he begins a digreſſion,——from that moment, I obſerve, his whole work ſtands ſtock-ſtill;——and if he goes on with his main work,——then there is an end of his digreſſion.

——This is vile work.—For which reaſon, from the beginning of this, you ſee, I have conſtructed the main work and the adventitious parts of it with ſuch interſections, and have ſo complicated and involved the digreſſive and progeſ-ſive movements, one wheel within ano-ther, that the whole machine, in general, has been kept a-going;——and, what's more, it ſhall be kept a-going theſe forty years, if it pleaſes the fountain of health to bleſs me ſo long with life and good ſpirits.

CHAP.

CHAP. XXIII.

I Have a ſtrong propenſity in me to begin this chapter very nonſenſically, and I will not balk my fancy.——Accordingly I ſet off thus.

If the fixure of *Momus*'s glaſs, in the human breaſt, according to the propoſed emendation of that arch-critick, had taken place,——firſt, This fooliſh conſequence would certainly have followed,—— That the very wiſeſt and the very graveſt of us all, in one coin or other, muſt have paid window-money every day of our lives.

And, ſecondly, That had the ſaid glaſs been there ſet up, nothing more would have been wanting, in order to have taken

ken

ken a man's character, but to have taken a chair and gone foftly, as you would
to a dioptrical bee-hive, and look'd in;—
view'd the foul ftark naked ;—obferv'd
all her motions,—her machinations ;—
traced all her maggots from their firft
engendering to their crawling forth ;—
watched her loofe in her frifks, her gam-
bols, her capricios ; and ofter fome notice of her more folemn deportment, con-
fequent upon fuch frifks, &c.——then
taken your pen and ink and fet down
nothing but what you had feen, and
could have fworn to :—But this is an
advantage not to be had by the bio-
grapher in this planet,—in the planet
Mercury (belike) it may be fo, if not
better ftill for him;——for there the in-
terffe heat of the country, which is pro-
ved by computators, from its vicinity to
the fun, to be more than equal to that
of

of red hot iron,—muſt, I think, long ago have vitrified the bodies of the inhabi-tants, (as the efficient cauſe) to ſuit them for the climate (which is the final cauſe) ; ſo that, betwixt them both, all the tene-ments of their ſouls, from top to bot-tom, may be nothing elſe, for aught the ſoundeſt philoſophy can ſhew to the con-trary, but one fine tranſparent body of clear glaſs (bating the umbilical knot);— ſo, that till the inhabitants grow old and tolerably wrinkled, whereby the rays of light, in paſſing through them, become ſo monſtrouſly refracted,——or return reflected from their ſurfaces in ſuch tranſverſe lines to the eye, that a man cannot be ſeen thro' ;—his ſoul might as well, unleſs, for more ceremony,—or the trifling advantage which the umbi-lical point gave her,—might, upon all

L 4 other

other accounts, I fay, as well play the
fool out o'doors as in her own houfe.

But this, as I faid above, is not the
cafe of the inhabitants of this earth ;—
our minds fhine not through the body,
but are wrapt up here in a dark covering
of uncryftalized flefh and blood ; fo that
if we would come to the fpecifick characters of them, we muft go fome other
way to work.

Many, in good truth, are the ways
which human wit has been forced to take
to do this thing with exactnefs.

Some, for inftance, draw all their characters with wind inftruments.—*Virgil*
takes notice of that way in the affair of
Dido and *Æneas* ;—but it is as fallacious
as the breath of fame ;—and, moreover,
be-

befpeaks a narrow genius. I am not ignorant that the *Italians* pretend to a mathematical exactnefs in their defignations
of one particular fort of character among
them, from the *forte* or *piano* of a certain wind inftrument they ufe,—which
they fay is infallible.—I dare not mention the name of the inftrument in this
place;—'tis fufficient we have it amongft
us,—but never think of making a drawing by it ;—this is ænigmatical, and intended to be fo, at leaft, *ad populum :*—
And therefore I beg, Madam, when you
come here, that you read on as faft as
you can, and never ftop to make any in-
quiry about it.

There are others again, who will draw
a man's character from no other helps in
the world, but merely from his evacua-
tions ;—but this often gives a very in-
correct

correct out-line,—unlefs, indeed, you
take a fketch of his repletions too; and
by correcting one drawing from the
other, compound one good figure out of
them both.

I fhould have no objection to this me-
thod, but that I think it muft fmell too
ftrong of the lamp,—and be render'd ftill
more operofe, by forcing you to have an
eye to the reft of his *Non-Naturals*.———
Why the moft natural actions of a man's
life fhould be call'd his Non-Naturals,—
is another queftion.

There are others, fourthly, who dif-
dain every one of thefe expedients;—not
from any fertility of his own, but from
the various ways of doing it, which they
have borrowed from the honourable de-
vices

vices which the Pentagraphic Brethren *
of the brush have shewn in taking co-
pies.—These, you must know, are your
great historians.

One of these you will see drawing a
full-length character *against the light*;—
that's illiberal,—dishonest,—and hard
upon the character of the man who sits.

Others, to mend the matter, will make
a drawing of you in the *Camera*;—that
is most unfair of all,—because, *there* you
are sure to be represented in some of
your most ridiculous attitudes.

To avoid all and every one of these
errors, in giving you my uncle *Toby*'s
character, I am determin'd to draw it by

no

---

* Pentagraph, an instrument to copy prints and
pictures mechanichally, and in any proportion.

4

no mechanical help whatever;———nor
fhall my pencil be guided by any one
wind inftrument which ever was blown
upon, either on this, or on the other
fide of the *Alps*;—nor will I confider
either his repletions or his difcharges,—
or touch upon his Non-Naturals;—but,
in a word, I will draw my uncle *Toby*'s
character from his HOBBY-HORSE.

C H A P. XXIV.

IF I was not morally fure that the reader
muft be out of all patience for my
uncle *Toby*'s character,——I would here
previoufly have convinced him, that
there is no inftrument fo fit to draw fuch
a thing with, as that which I have pitch'd
upon.

A

A man and his HOBBY-HORSE,
tho' I cannot fay that they act and re-act
exactly after the fame manner in which
the foul and body do upon each other :
Yet doubtlefs there is a communication
between them of fome kind, and my
opinion rather is, that there is fomething
in it more of the manner of electrified
bodies,—and that by means of the heated
parts of the rider, which come immediately into contact with the back of the
HOBBY-HORSE.—By long journies and
much friction, it fo happens that the body of the rider is at length fill'd as full
of HOBBY-HORSICAL matter as it can
hold ;——fo that if you are able to give
but a clear defcription of the nature of
the one, you may form a pretty exact
notion of the genius and character of the
other.

- Now

Now the Hobby-Horse which my
uncle *Toby* always rode upon, was, in my
opinion, an Hobby-Horse well worth
giving a defcription of, if it was only
upon the fcore of his great fingularity;
for you might have travelled from *York*
to *Dover*,——from *Dover* to *Penzance* in
Cornwall, and from *Penzance* to *York* back
again, and not have feen fuch another
upon the road; or if you had feen fuch
a one, whatever hafte you had been in,
you muft infallibly have ftopp'd to have
taken a view of him. Indeed, the gait
and figure of him was fo ftrange, and fo
utterly unlike was he, from his head to
his tail, to any one of the whole fpecies,
that it was now and then made a matter
of difpute,——whether he was really a
Hobby-Horse or no: But as the Philofopher would ufe no other argument to
the fceptic, who difputed with him againft
the

the reality of motion, fave that of rifing up upon his legs, and walking a-crofs the room ;—fo would my uncle *Toby* ufe no other argument to prove his HOBBY; HORSE was a HOBBY-HORSE indeed, but by getting upon his back and riding him about;—leaving the world after that to determine the point as it thought fit.

In good truth, my uncle *Toby* mounted him with fo much pleafure, and he car-ried my uncle *Toby* fo well,——that he troubled his head very little with what the world either faid or thought about it.

It is now high time, however, that I give you a defcription of him :—But to go on regularly, I only beg you will give me leave to acquaint you firft, how my uncle *Toby* came by him.

C H A P.

C H A P. XXV.

THE wound in my uncle *Toby*'s groin, which he received at the fiege of *Namur*, rendering him unfit for the fervice, it was thought expedient he fhould return to *England*, in order, if poffible, to be fet to rights.

He was four years totally confined,— part of it to his bed, and all of it to his room; and in the courfe of his cure, which was all that time in hand, fuffer'd unfpeakable miferies,—owing to a fuc-ceffion of exfoliations from the *ofs pubis*, and the outward edge of that part of the *coxendix* called the *ofs illeum*,———both which bones were difmally crufh'd, as much by the irregularity of the ftone, which I told you was broke off the pa-

rapet,

rapet,—as by its fize,—(though it was
pretty large) which inclined the furgeon
all along to think, that the great injury
which it had done my uncle *Toby*'s groin,
was more owing to the gravity of the
ftone itfelf, than to the projectile force
of it,—which he would often tell him
was a great happinefs.

My father at that time was juft beginning bufinefs in *London*, and had taken a
houfe ;—and as the trueft friendfhip and
cordiality fubfifted between the two bro-
thers,—and that my father thought my
uncle *Toby* could no where be fo well
nurfed and taken care of as in his own
houfe,——he affign'd him the very beft
apartment in it.—And what was a much
more fincere mark of his affection ftill,
he would never fuffer a friend or an ac-
quaintance to ftep into the houfe on any

occafion, but he would take him by the hand, and lead him up ftairs to fee his brother *Toby*, and chat an hour by his bed fide.

The hiftory of a foldier's wound beguiles the pain of it;—my uncle's vifiters at leaft thought fo, and in their daily calls upon him, from the courtefy arifing out of that belief, they would frequently turn the difcourfe to that fubject,—and from that fubject the difcourfe would generally roll on to the fiege itfelf.

Thefe converfations were infinitely kind; and my uncle *Toby* received great relief from them, and would have received much more, but that they brought him into fome unforefeen perplexities, which, for three months together, retarded his cure greatly; and if he had

not

not hit upon an expedient to extricate himſelf out of them, I verily believe they would have laid him in his grave.

What theſe perplexities of my uncle *Toby* were,——'tis impoſſible for you to gueſs ;—if you could,—I ſhould bluſh ; not as a relation,—not as a man,—nor even as a woman,—but I ſhould bluſh as an author ; inaſmuch as I ſet no ſmall ſtore by myſelf upon this very account, that my reader has never yet been able to gueſs at any thing. And in this, Sir, I am of ſo nice and ſingular a humour, that if I thought you was able to form the leaſt judgment or probable conjecture to yourſelf, of what was to come in the next page,—I would tear it out of my book.

END of the FIRST VOLUME.

177